AF531539

Environmental Deprivation and Perceptual Tasks of Pre-school Children

Dr. T. Kalyani Devi

Department of Human Development & Family Studies
S.P. Mahila Visvavidyalayam
Tirupati — 517 502

DISCOVERY PUBLISHING HOUSE
NEW DELHI – 110 002

Published by :

Discovery Publishing House
4831/24, Ansari Road, Prahlad Street
Darya Ganj, New Delhi–110 002 (INDIA)
Phone : 327 9245
Fax : 91–11–3253475

First Published—1998
Reprinted-2011

ISBN 81–7141–440–0

Laser Typeset by :

Allied Computers,
Karnal (Haryana)

Mehra Offset Press
Delhi

Foreword

I am pleased that T. Kalyani Devi, is publishing a book entitled "Environmental Deprivation and Perceptual Tasks of Pre-school Children" based on her research studies on the effects of environmental deprivation on simple perceptual tasks of pre-school children.

The scenario of pre-school age children especially growing up in rural areas of our country is not altogether satisfactory because of poor, impoverished and low quality perceptual inputs.

Though a number of studies have been published focussing upon the causal relationship between environment and cognitive growth in children, the contents of this book throw new light on the specific aspects of perceptual ability using innovative test materials. Therefore, I consider this book as exceedingly relevant and useful to researchers in the areas of human development and family studies as well as post-graduate students of human development, psychology and social work.

It is unfortunate that a large number of children of pre-school years not only live in homes which lack optimum level of quality of perceptual stimulation but also go to schools which do not provide sufficiently adequate perceptual stimulation. This is very much true in the case of rural schools including anganwadies and balwadis. Thus the children live and grow in an interlocked situation wherein neither home nor school provides a reasonably good quality of perceptual stimulation. It is natural that the perceptual development of such children gets adversely affected. No one seems to recognised this fact sufficiently seriously. There is a great need to enrich the quality of perceptual stimulation in preschools so that the child's perceptual development becomes satisfactory. The results presented in this Book emphatically support this view and call for scientifically designing the perceptual inputs and monitoring the quality over a long period. Taking care of the nutritional aspects alone will not be enough to meet the total growth needs of the children. Though this is accepted by all, in practice the role of perceptual inputs into the child's environment has been rather neglected.

I hope this book will be read and appreciated by cognate experts and workers in the area of child development and provide enriched perceptual inputs.

I congratulate T. Kalyani Devi for arranging publication of her research studies in the thrust area of human development studies. I also thank the publisher for bringing the material in the form of a book for researching a larger section of readers.

I am sure this book will be well received and found useful.

Prof. S.R. Venkatramaiah
Retired Dean
School of Biological and Eart h Sciences
Sri Venkateswara University Tirupati

Contents

1
Introduction

A large number of children in pre-school years growing up in developing countries seem to suffer a handicap in the form of a poor or impoverished environmental facility. To live and grow up in such a disadvantaged position means a definite underdevelopment of some of the basic skills necessary to interact affectively later in life. No one would disagree at present that malnutrition affects the normal growth and development of children. Philip, E., Vernon (1972) rightly observes, "..... It is not only the poor circumstances of the parents but the back-wardness and resistance to charge which results in the under development of their child's capacities".

The interaction between cognitive growth & development and cultural environment seems to be better understood now than before. The work of Piaget (1950), Bruner (1966), Jensen (1972), Vernon (1972) and several others have brought clarity to the current conceptions of cognitive growth and development in relation to environment. We now know, for instance, that starting from a simple sensory motor reflexes at the time of birth, a succession of more complex and adaptive skills are systematically built up through the impact of environmental stimulation on the child's maturing nervous system as well as through its active exploration and experiments. Thus, a series of stages of successive reorganizations are recognised in the child's perception, speech and thinking through which children progress at different rates. It is no longer disputable that children who are disadvantaged progress in a typically different fashion than others do without such a disadvantage.

Vernon (1972) lists some eleven positive environmental factors which seem to influence cognitive ability. Some of the important ones are:

1. Reasonable satisfaction of biological and social needs, including exercise and curiosity.
2. Varied stimulation, encouragement of exploration, experiment and play (Perceptual and Kinaesthetic experience).
3. Linguistic stimulation.
4. 'Demanding' but 'democratic' family climate, emphasizing infernal controls and responsibility.
5. Conceptual stimulation by rich environment books, travel etc.

Introduction of pre-school education programmes and child welfare services in the community no doubt have gone a long way in attacking the syndrome of negative influence of a backward culture and poverty, on healthy development in children.

There is a growing evidence to show that cultural deprivation retards development particularly cognitive development. Therefore it is reasonable to expect culturally deprived children to find it difficult to cope with the demands of schooling. Such children may have to be dealt with by specially designing appropriate programmes, compensating for the harmful effects of deprivation.

Fundamentally, a child growing up in a poor environment lacks the richness of perceptual stimulation and experience available to the child growing up in a relatively superior environment. Poor performance on standard tests and under achievement of such children may be attributed to this single factor. However we do not have conclusive evidence to support the exact manner in which poor environment mediates or gets involved casually with such an *end state*. For instance, questions such as, the following, could be raised,

1. What kind of experience or lack of it, is *critical* in the normal cognitive growth with special reference to perceptual skills?
2. How do the cultural components of environm nt i ter-act and determine the perceptual efficiency in a *growing* child?
3. Are there *culture specific* determinants for such deviations in perceptual efficiency?

The present investigation is a attempt to examine these, issues by empirically studying the performance of *selected children* on a simple perceptual task requiring discrimination of form and colour.

An attempt is made to discuss briefly some of the major theoretical formulations and issues concerning the relevant aspects of cognitive growth and development in children, to serve as a background.

Some Basic Theoretical Approaches

There are several attempts to formulate a theory of development of cognitive functions during the childhood. We notice three distinct trends in theory construction namely, the *genetic functionalistic approach, the comparative developmental approach* and *environmental cultural approach* (Sociological) emphasizing the development of representation system in the individual.

Some of the theoretical formulations, to be discussed incorporate one or more of the above approaches and thus a midway between the extremes.

Piaget (1963) and his co-workers have formulated what is considered as the most systematic and comprehensive theory of cognitive growth based on naturalistic and scientific observational studies. Central to this theory, is the convincing empirical evidence to establish "*stage dependent invariant order of development*". It is presumed that there is an active process where perceptual experience (categories) represents the general manner in which they are related as a results of interaction between the child and the external world. In the beginning these representations are in the form of simple structures and gradually get transformed through assimilation and accommodation, to more complex structures. This is a process of an orderly sequence of stages. It is admitted, that though invariant, this order or sequence may be accelerated or slowed down, due to social and cultural influences, but the sequence itself remains unalterable. As can be seen, this theory is a biologically oriented and deals with the development as coming to terms with environment in terms of the ability to cope with it. The sequence of cognitive development is described as follows.

1. Sensori motor stage—birth to 2 or 3 years
2. Pre operational thinking—2 or 3 to 7 or 8 years
3. Concrete operation—7 or 8 to 11 or 12 years
4. Formal operation—11 or 12 to 14 or 15 years.

Piaget, conceptualizes different levels of cognitive development in terms of differences in the qualitative nature of cognitive process and emergence of new ones. Even though a new stage emerges at certain points in cognitive growth there is a continuity in the sequence of changes with certain unique structural characteristics at each stage. It is very important for any one dealing with children to identify these unique characteristics at each level, so that the children can be effectively managed.

The recent work which marks a revival of interest in piaget show that cognitive changes can be caused as a result of interaction between the method of training and the content area involved at the particular developmental level of child. This is perhaps one of the most important implications to curriculum planning and teaching strategies to be employed in teaching disadvantaged children.

Bruner (1966) approaches the studies in cognitive growth in a slightly different manner from the Piaget. Though he speaks of progress through qualitatively different stages, he distinguishes three main levels of processing information. He calls them *inactive*, the *iconic* and the *symbolic*, In the *enactive* stage the child acquires the capacity to move around to grasp etc., which helps the child in understanding space at this stage. At the *iconic* stage of the child understands the world in terms of percepts and images of a concrete kind. However the child is unable to relate this to one another. The third stage namely, *symbolic*, is a more general and abstract concept of the world interms of words, numbers and ideas. There is conservation phenomena. Bruner's description of cognitive growth has brought clarity to our understanding of children growing up in backward societies. It is familiar that children living in backward societies learn through doing than through words, they imitate older children and adults and thus form concepts of the world around them.

Jensen (1973) has put forward what is considered as a novel conception that environment affects development mainly as a "*threasold variable*". He argues that environment operates like diet in relation to *physical growth.* This kind of argument has aroused a great deal of controversy in the area of cultural different in the growth of abilities. Jensen has shown that conventional tests of intelligence probably give better indications of allround learning ability in middle class children than in lower class children. He speaks of two types of abilities namely, *associated ability* and *cognitive ability*, which are independent in so far as they underline genetic aspects. The former measure the *breadth* aspects of ability while the latter describes the *altitude* aspects of the ability. In terms of the mental function, information and vocabulary are related to breadth. Problem solving and reasoning are related to the altitude, what is affected by environment and training is the breadth aspect of the ability. One of the most significant aspects of this approach is the relationship between socio-cultural aspects and intelligence. Jensen, expresses himself in favour of a largely genetic explanation of the evidence on racial and social group differences in educational performance. He certainly does not favour the orthodox view that all behavioural variation between groups is due to cultural differences, social discrimination and inequalities of opportunity.

Werner (1947) believes in a common development principles. The similarity between cognitive process of primitive people and immature children is the focal point. Werner provides a wealth of evidence from across the different regions of the world in support of his theory of mental development. Both the primitive people and immature children show diffused undifferentiated thinking, animism magical thinking, and concretism. In contrast, civilized people and mature children show articulation, organised abstracts thinking. Even in this approach, stages are not totally excluded. The development is regarded as a progress in an orderly and specificable fashion from a state of relative generality to a state of increasing differentiation. The arguments concerning the pattern of cognitive development, mentioned above, have made a deep impact on research studies, specially dealing with cultural factors involved.

Vernon (1970) has brought greater clarity into the intricate problem of cultural environment and cognitive and intellectual growth. He has explored the role of environment and other factors which hinders the development of abilities within under-developed countries or minority groups. As a preliminary to this very influential work, he has redefined the cognitive ability by identifying three different meanings associated with the term. He speaks of intelligence A, B and C emphasizing the genetic foundation, the cumulative affects of the interaction with the environment and the measured ability of a child on a standard test. In comparing different cultural groups one has to give appropriate consideration to each one of these type. Vernon has gathered evidence by extensive surveys and experimental studies on the relationship between environmental influence and growth of cognitive and intellectual ability. It is reported that differences between type B and C mentioned above within a cultural group are largely genetically determined. However when environmental differences are more extreme their affects become very prominent. Some major environmental factors which have a positive influence on mental development are

1. Nutritional and Health conditions
2. Perceptual and sensori-motor experiences
3. Language
4. Child rearing practices and parental attitudes.

Perceptual Development in Children with Special References to Form and Colour

Perceptual Development on par with other perhaps more obvious aspects of child behaviour, is also subjected to important changes during the course of growth and development. A complete understanding of the development of behaviour of childhood, requires therefore, a concern with the process of mechanisms underlying the development of perceptual skills and judgements, many of which are intimately related to learning, thinking and motivation. The relationship between environment, sensory experience and perceptual development is direct and most important, from the point of view of total psychological adjustment of children. Absence of sensory experience leads to deprivation resulting in severe blocking of perceptual development. Children who are congenitally blind and or deaf suffer most in this respect. Therefore, the importance of the area of sensory-perceptual process to intellectual-cognitive development is at once obvious. It is perhaps relevant state that social adequacy of perceptual process is meaningfully related to cognitive ability.

Trends in Perceptual Development

The study of perceptual development is fundamental to understand the child's ability to deal with the environment. It involves identification and discrimination of forms, colours, size and space which constitute the principal components of the external world. Some of the basic questions involved in this area are;

1. What is the earliest age in which the child is able to identify and discriminate objects in terms of the components mentioned above?
2. What are the trends in the growth of the perceptual ability?
3. What factors influence the perceptual development?

Form and Colour.

Form discriminations are among the first if not the very first, shown by the growing child. Fantz (1958) has shown that the consistent preferences for visual patterns are present as early as the first two months of life. Form discriminations were found to be present as early as sixth month, Ling (1941). Further he has pointed out that changes in relative position, spatial orientation, or size of either or both positive and negative stimulation has very slight effect on the discrimination performance of the child.

A comparative study in perceptual development between primates and children were attempted to establish differences in the rate of growth (Gellerman, 1933 and Weinstein, 1941). It was generally found that human subjected *vis a vis* age, performed better than primates on perceptual discrimination tasks.

Both form and colour concepts are developed early in the child's life. Up to the age of three the children showed a marked tendency to choose form as a basis for matchings. From three to six years of age, colour becomes the most potent factor. After age six to adult life, form again becomes the predominating factor in the subject's choices. At the adult level about 90 percent of the matching were made on the basis of form. In an attempt to explain cyclical nature of their findings, the investigators indulged in some interesting speculations. They reasoned that when the child begins to develop concepts, the abstraction are of the *genus* rather than that of species type. The child looks for the most common features among objects. All men become 'Daddy', all time pieces become tick-tock' and so forth. In making these early differentiations (form) functions are of primary importance and colour can usually be ignored. "A rose is a rose" whether white, yellow, or red. After the child has developed some facility in making these gross genus classifications (at about three years), colour becomes an important factor in making species classifications within a particular genus. A red cow is a different animal from a black cow at this age. At a still later age from six years to maturity there is a gradual shift back to form as the most potent factor because children have mastered the fundamentals of genus-species classifications.

The children of the kindergarten age can be influenced to choose in a matching situation on the basis of colour by making the colour differences very large or on the basis of form by making the form differences very pronounced, (Hung, 1945).

Crudden (1941) reported that the children of primary school are able to abstract a known figure from a relatively unknown configurations. He has also found that the girls were superior to boys in this type of abstraction ability.

That the updown of orientation of the letters p & g as compared with b & d was not significant to prevent confusion and lack of discrimination before a mental age of six years, and the left right orientation of letters b and d was not discriminated adequately until a seven and one-half year mental age (Davidson 1935).

At all ages, children like colour. What colour they like and how saturated they like them will depend mainly upon the child's age. The younger the child, the better he likes colours which are bold and saturated. No colour is too bright to please him, whether it be used to clothing or toys or merely as a sample in a test. Pastel shades and subdued hues are perceived as ugly by the young children. With increasing age, however, this attitude changes. By adolescence, both boys and girls show a marked tendency to prefer the duller shades and less saturated hues, and they regard the saturated colours as loud or hideous. Most children prefer blue, red and green to all other colours, black white, yellow and orange are least liked. Boys prefer red, while girls prefer blue and violet.

Form and colour concepts are among the first developed for functional use during childhood. There is steady increase in the ability to perceive and use colour correctly and also there is a steady increase in colour discrimination among others (Hurlock and Thomson 1934).

Colour matching and colour naming abilities are increased with age, colour discrimination ability is considerably more advanced than colour naming. Children of each age can discriminate more accurately between differences in hue (red, green, yellow and so forth) than between differences in brightness or saturation (Cook, 1931).

The question of relative salience of form and colour at a given age is extensively studied. Some of the interesting findings are (a) responsiveness to colour represents a more primitive mode of functioning than responsiveness to form. There is a general increase in form salience with age (Kagan & Lemkin 1961). (b) Within a age group subjects preferring form to colours are found to be more adaptive than those who prefer colour. (c) there is an initial decline in form preference followed by increase in colour salience (Melkman & Koriat 1976). The development of colour-form salience in Pre-schoolers appears to reflect variations in environmental contingences. Two explanations have been suggested for this phenomena. There is a common underlying process for the initial decline in colour preference and subsequent raise in form preference. There is perhaps cognitive and emotional correlates operating in the form preference in young children.

Influence of Family, Social Class and Deprivation

Among the several factors, that might influence perceptual development in children, the most important ones appear to be *the family, the social class and deprivation*, which either independently or together may influence perceptual development. The interest is family life *variables* as an important source is of recent origin. The following are some of the important aspects of family life variable which need to be carefully studied.

Parental Background

This includes educational, occupational and personality characteristics of parents.

Family Status and Composition

The social class status, size, type, etc., are some of the relevant aspects.

Interpersonal Relations Within the Family

In this area power relations, sharing and cooperation, communication, and decision making patterns are included.

Parental Attitudes and Beliefs

This specially refers to child rearing goals parental involvement, attitudes to discipline etc.,

There appears to be no specific studies on the influence of one or the other above mentioned variables on perceptual development in children. However there are a few studies examining the influence of social class and deprivation on cognitive development in children, both in our country and outside. These studies will be reviewed in the next chapter.

Poverty may influence the process of development of cognitive functioning. Lower socio-economic class children for instance, fail on tasks which demand verbal ability, reasoning, number facility and space conceptualisation (Lesser, Filfer & Clark 1965). This explains the harmful effect of poverty. Coington (1967) who studied stimulus deprivation as a function of social class membership found that children of low socio-economic status were poor in discrimination tasks. Tripathi & Misra (1975, 1976) reported that the prolonged deprivation has negative relationship with cognitive efficiency. Rao, (1976) revealed that high Socio economic status and high income help the development of cognitive competence.

Children's achievement over perceptual activities are to be based on their antecedent factors like sex, religion, caste, income, parents education, occupation and leisure time activities (Sundeep 1978). Lack of visual perceptual skills and field articulation also may result due to cultural deprivation. Protein calorie malnutrition prevents the development of higher cognitive competence (Levinsky 1977). Home environment may also influence the child's perceptual tasks. School is the most influential factor in the cognitive development.

Recent studies have shown that the type of instruction and organisational structure of a school is condencive to significant and consistent success over government schools, that too rural based schools, on the perceptual organisations and spatial orientation tasks. Other investigators reported that the differences in intelligence and scholastic achievement increase with the degree of social disadvantage. A study of the influence of age, schooling and socio-economic factors on the development of certain perceptual skills revealed that caste status and equality of school affected the performance in perception (Sandeep 1978 & Pushpa, 1980).

Parent child interaction is yet another factor that plays a vital role in cognitive development. Low parental encouragement, low education, lower motivation, lack of identification and less interaction with adults results in cognitive deficiencies.

Age

Age is one of the most important factors studied in perceptual development of children. The individual differences are a rule rather than exception in developing countries. Bernreuter (1953) pointed out that ".... As the child gets older, more specific factors emerge, so that by the time he is adult, mental activity is analyzable into specific factors, and the general factor is little importance.." In other words, as the age increases, the more specific abilities of the child are differentiated progressively.

Developmental studies have consistently reported a gradual increase in form salience with age (Brain & Good enough, 1929; Kagan & Lemkin 1961). With increasing age a decreasing preference for high saturation, an increasing consisting of hue choice compared with consistency of saturation choices, and an increasing tendency to resolves conflicts in favour of huc rather than saturation (Irvin (1968). Some studies reported no significant differences in colour form preferences by age.

Sex

Most of the studies (kagan 1961, Irvin 1968 & Olmsted 1972) on the influence of sex on perceptual development have reported that the sex differences are not significant in perceptual development.

Social Class

Immediate Social Environment

Early social interaction, particularly, mother-infant interaction has been recognised as an important determiner or correlate both for affective and cognitive development. Klaus, Knnel, Plumb and Zuehlke (1970) have shown that the early maternal behaviour toward and premature is attenuated compared to the interaction of the mother with a full term baby. Kagan, Wimberger, and Bobbitt (1969) have suggested that the mother-child interaction of retarded three to seven year old is more neutral and less active than for non-retarded four to five year old. The parent child transactions are determined by unique characteristics of the child as well as social cognition. The influence is felt on language as well as social cognition.

Social-Cultural Environment

Documentation for the social-cultural factors has come from Heber (1973). He has identified a disproportionate number of persons labeled as retarded because of low socio-economic and or ethnic minority backgrounds. Heber (1973) have demonstrated a significant improvement is measured intelligence of developmentally retarded infants in a high risk sample. This improvement followed systematic rearing and stimulating interventions during the first few years of life. Low socio-economic background interacts with retarded infant development resulting in disproportionate. I.Q. deficits in later development. Tulkin (1972) notes three main reasons for cultural deprivation.

1. The concept of cultural deprivation does not advance science or knowledge because it focuses on presuming the effects of conditions which are absent and often

overlooks the importance of the processes by which actual and specific environmental experiences influence development.

2. The concept of cultural deprivation ignores cultural relativism and fails to respect multicultural differences, some of which may have developed as means of coping with the effects of poverty and hard times.
3. Finally the concept of cultural deprivation neglects the political realities which are largely responsible for many of the traits observed in disadvantaged population.

An Over View

We may make some pertinent observations from the foregoing discussion on basic concepts, approaches and factors influencing the perceptual development in children. There are fundamental discoveries with regard to the stage dependent, sequences in cognitive growth and development in children. Disregarding certain minor variations in the definitions of stages, the main import of existing literature is to focus on the child's ability to deal with the environment, in which it lives and grows. The facility of a rich environment is necessary for maximum development of the potential.

In developing countries children seem to suffer a major handicap of poor environmental facility and hence suffer, less than maximum cognitive growth and development. There is a need for more data on the trends in perceptual development of children growing up in impoverished environment. Form and colour are the most fundamental components of visual experience. We need to have research information, on the discrimination of both these components, in relation to one's own environment. This information is helpful in designing appropriate experiences for children attending pre-schools in rural and urban areas.

The general objective of pre-schools is to create an environment suitable for the social, emotional, physical and intellectual development. The other objectives of a preschool education is to give opportunities for learning basic skills. A good pre-school should provide opportunity for the child to develop desirable social attitudes, emotional maturity, aesthetic appreciation and the feeling of independence and creativity.

The pre-school experience supplements and enriches the basic experience that a home offers. Because in the pre-school, children are encouraged to broaden their horizons, to develop new interests, to experience the stimulation and satisfaction of exploring, manipulating, and creating. They discover people-people interactions of their own age to play with and adults who like and respect them. They gain confidence in meeting new situations, adjusting to people, and finding that a first step towards maturity is an exciting adventure.

The present investigation has as its main aim to study the effects of prolonged deprivation on form and colour discrimination performance of pre-school age children. The results of such a study are expected to give insight into nature of visual experience of children in pre-school education programmes.

2

Review of Extant Literature

The extant literature on perceptual development in children in considerably vast and numerous. Many fundamental aspects related to perception in children have been extensively studied. In this review an attempt is made to present the findings of research investigation on perceptual development in children with particular reference to colour and form. Our interest is to focus not so much on the basic trends as much as it is to focus on cross cultural comparisons in relations to the influence of environment. The reasons being, that we have very little information on the influence of poor environment as it exists in relatively deprived social conditions on cognitive abilities of children. For the sake of convenience, it is proposed to present the review under two broad headings namely;

A. Studies on developmental trends in the perceptual of colour and form during early childhood and,

B. Studies on the specific effects of environmental variables and prolonged deprivation on the performance of children on perceptual tasks.

A. Studies on Development Trends in the Perception of Colour and Form during Early Childhood

The earliest study on relative potency of colour and form perception is that of Brain and Goodenough (1929). The sample consisted of the children of 2 to 14 years of age plus 40 adult women. The subjects were required to choose between the two alternatives of colour and form in matching a series of three objects. There was equal opportunity to match on the basis of either colour or form but the subject had to make a choice. The results showed that up to the age of three years' the children showed a marked tendency to choose form as a basis for matching; from three to six years of age, colour becomes the most potent factor in the subjects' choices. At the adult level about 90 percent of the matchings were made on the basis of form.

Rice, (1930) studied the orientation of plane figures as a factor in the perception by children. The sample consisted of 26 children. The age range was 2 years 7 months and 9 years 3 months. He presented two identical figures (diamonds, spoons and others) not in the same position. The children were required to recognize two differently oriented figures which were identically same. The results showed that the ability to recognise 'Sameness' by some word or action between two differently oriented figures appears rather than suddenly between the ages of five and six. It is not clearly explained why there is such a sudden transition. It is suggested that the body image is perhaps necessary for a proper perception of direction and hence the position of objects in the space.

A comparative study of development of a perception of form, between human begins and primates, has been undertaken to find out the relative superiority in terms of maturation. Gellerman (1933), for example, investigated the relative ability of primates and two year old children in discriminating triangularity perse. The results showed the two year old children can discriminate triangularity *per se* (regardless of position, size and background) more adequately than primates.

Crudden (1941) studied the form abstraction by children. He selected 65 to 78 months age children for the study. The children had to discriminate eight pairs of geometrical figures. His results showed that primary school children were able "to abstract a known figure from a relatively unknown configuration. Girls, were found to be superior to boys in this type of abstraction ability. This reflects the general acceleration noticed in girls in verbal concept formation.

Form discrimination as a learning cue in infants was studied by Ling (1941). Fifty children between 6 and 15 months of age were studied. They were presented with two or more blocks differing shape (circle, cross, triangle and others). The incorrect forms were fasterned to the presentation board, while the correct forms were sweetened with sacharine. The results showed that the discrimination of form *per se* was present as early as the six month of life. Change in the relative position, spatial orientation, or size either or both positive and negative stimuli had only slight effect on the discrimination performance of the infants. It appears that as early as the sixth month of life, some concept of form would have developed, that is; at least independent of obsolute size. This study has confirmed the presence of form discrimination even among infants.

Ability to copy forms in pre-school children was studied by Graham, Berman and Bernhart (1960). The sample consisted of 108 children, 18 in each of six age groups, proceeding by half-year steps from two and a half years to five years. In each half-year age group, there were 9 boys and 9 girls, of whom 3 of each sex were Negro and 6 were white. Each subject was tested individually. The stimuli consisted of 18 forms. They were drawn in India ink on 5" x 8" white cards, with one design to a card. There were three curvilinear drawings. The remainder were line drawings. Two methods of conceptualizing developmental changes were contrasted a continuity point of view emphasizing qualitative organisations typical of a particular stage of development, and a continuity point of view emphasizing quantitative changes in the accuracy of reproduction. To test whether specified qualitative organisations characterized the reproductions, each reproduction was judged as to whether it showed a change from the original in being more "primitive" or more non-primitive. Three characteristics of primitive organisation simplification, closure, and increased symmetry and their logical opposites were judged. The major findings failed to confirm the predictions of this theoretical point of view. Simplification and closure were found to be more common in the reproductions of younger than of older children but they were no more common than the opposite characteristics of complicating and opening. Both pairs of characteristics declined with age, and the decline was not differential. Increasing the symmetry of a reproduction was more common than decreasing the symmetry only in the three and one-half year group. The interaction with age was, however, significant.

Kagan and Lemkin (1961) conducted a study on form, colour and size in children's conceptual behaviour. This study described an experiment on the conceptual preferences of children when they were asked to group geometric stimuli differing in form, colour or size into similar pairs. The subjects selected for the study 35 boys and 35 girls (ages 3 years 9 months and 8 years 6 months). The children were presented with nine stimuli in which a standard stimulus was presented simultaneously with other stimuli differing in form, colour and size. The child was asked to select the comparison stimulus which was the "same as " the standard. The results indicated that for both boys and girls, form was distinctively preferred to colour as a basis for similarity and that colour was preferred over size. For boys there was no age differences in this response pattern. However older girls were less likely than younger girls to use colour as the basis for conceptualization. Older boys moreover, were more likely to use colour than were the older girls. The sex differences between older boys and girls were difficult to explain. One post hoc argument is presented. Since the verbal skills of young girls proceed precociously in relation to boys, it is possible that the girls implicitly apply the language labels, square, triangle, circle to the stimuli more often than boys. Thus for the girls, the stimuli are more likely to derive their meaning from the label attached to them rather than through the more direct physical quality of colour.

The results of the study does not clearly answer the question of form and colour salience in relation to age. There is however a suggestion that at all ages form has more potency over colour, and colour over size. The age versus colour and form preference in the case of girls has revealed interaction effect.

Gibson, and Gibson, Pick and Osser (1962) made an attempt to study development of the discrimination of letter like forms in children. This experiment studied qualitatively as well as quantitatively the development of visual discrimination of letter like forms in children (4-8 years). The forms were constructed according to the same constraints which govern formation of printed capitals, 12 were chosen as capitals 12 were chosen as standards and 12 specified, transformation were constructed for each standard. The transformations were three degree of changes from line to curve or *vice versa* five changes in orientation; two perspective transformations, and two topological transformations. The discrimination task required the child to match a standard form with an identical form. The experiment was repeated for the five years of old group using real letters (Capitals). The results showed that overall error scores decreased with age, but difficulty of discrimination was different for different transformations. Initial errors were greatest for perspective transformations and least for topological transformations, with changes of rotation and reversal in between changes of line to curve varied in difficulty depending on the number of changes. The four classes of transformation showed similarity of slope within the class, but significant differences were found between them. Errors made with real letters correlated significantly with errors made with letter-like forms.

Corah (1966) investigated the effects of instructional sets and performance sets on the colour-form perception. The sample of this study was 180 kindergarten children. Instructions stressing colour, form or neither dimension were used. Performance set was varied by presenting pretest tasks that emphasized colour, form or neither dimension. The results showed, instructional sets had little or no effect on colour-form matching. The control levels of response favoured form over colour. It was found that young children had a stronger tendency to match on the basis of colour.

The above studies have strongly pointed out the predominance of form over colour in matching task among pre-school age children, but one is not sure enough that such a tendency will persist among children, in different socio-cultural environment. If a definite preference for form is an evidence of high abstraction capacity, then the deprived children (disadvantaged) in contrast should show a preponderance or colour preference, other conditions being same.

The question of relative importance of touch and vision in shape perception in children was tackled by Deleon, Raskin and Grun (1970). Forty eight children between 3 to 4 years constituted the sample.. In addition, shape perception based on the integrated use of both touch and vision was studied. Visual discrimination was found to be superior to tactual discrimination in discriminating random forms. The integrated use of both touch and vision in shape discrimination resulted in no better performance than that of vision alone. An exploratory condition did suggest that visual exploration of a standard stimulus enhanced tactual discrimination. However this condition always occurred last and thus, is difficult to interpret because of practice effects.

This study is of particular interest because the phenomena of inter-sensory integration is discussed. It is surprising that experience of touch did not additionally facilitate shape discrimination through vision. Perhaps the shapes chosen had strong visual cues sufficient for maximal discrimination.

Siegel and Vance (1970) studied the visual and haptic dimensional preference. They selected 16 children of each of four grade levels, pre-schools, kindergarten, first grade and third grade. They were given dimensional preference task in both visual and haptic modalities, with three-dimensional stimuli varying in form, size and colour or texture. The results showed that the pattern of preference scores was essentially the same in both visual and haptic tasks. All age groups, except the pre-schoolers, showed marked form dominance. Form was especially salient for the kindergartners. Colours, texture and size preferences were relatively low at all ages.

Rajyalakshmi Muralidharan (1970) directed a nation wide study on developmental norms of Indian children between 2½ and 5 years. The sample consisted of 30 boys and 30 girls at every age level from 2½ to 5 years (2½, 3, 3½, 4, 4½ and 5 years) for the urban, rural and industrial areas of Ahmedabad, Alahabad, Bombay, Calcutta, Delhi, Hyderabad and Madras. The total sample examined 6977 children. For identification of colours red, blue, green, yellow, white and black were chosen. For form discrimination geometric forms (circle, square, triangle, cross etc.) were chosen. Cards of red, blue, green, yellow, white and black are presented to the child one by one with an aim to find out if he can discriminate and name the colours. In case he is unable to name the colours he is asked to identify the colours and in case he is not able to identify, he is asked to match the colour by presenting him with an additional card of one colour at a time. For form discrimination the child was asked to copy the different geometric forms (circle, square, triangle, cross etc.). The results reported are briefly summarised below

Circle

1. The pattern of copying a circle vary so much in terms of size, shape and direction that it is only seldom that predominant patterns emerge.
2. However, pattern's of copying circle get indicated from 3 to 3½ years in the majority of the urban groups and form 3½ to 4 years in the majority of the rural boys and industrial groups. In rural girls it occurs by 4 and 4½ years.
3. It is only the children of Calcutta who do it from 3 to 3½ years onwards, the rural children from 4½ years and industrial children 4 to 4½ years. The children from other centres are mostly found to draw oblong or misshapen circle.
4. Children of Calcutta and Hyderabad and the industrial children of Ahmedabad, the urban girls of Bombay and Madras, the rural girls of Madras and the industrial girls of Bombay are able to copy a circle approximately equal in size to the model. The majority of above groups are able to do it from 4 to 4½ years.
5. All groups of children except the children of Hyderabad draw the circle in clock wise direction. The children of Hyderabad, however, tend to do it in the anti-clock wise direction.

Square

1. The majority of the urban girls and industrial boys and girls start to indicate patterns of copying a square from 3½ years while the urban boys do so from 4 years and the rural boys and girls from 4½ years. However and 3½ years except for the children of Calcutta, the other industrial children and urban girls show either only partial pattern of copying or they draw misshapen figures. The rural children tend to do this right up to 5 years.
2. The majority of the urban children are able to make well defined corners from 4 years, from 4½ years they show a uniformity with reference to the direction viz., they start to make the vertical sides from top to bottom and the horizontal sides from left to right from 5 years they are able to copy a square of the same size as the model. In the case of children of Calcutta and other rural children do not show these

features within 5 years. The majority of the industrial children on the other hand show uniformity in direction, size and defining corners, only at 5 years.

Triangle

1. The urban and industrial children are found to be unable to copy the triangle upto 3 years and the rural children upto 3½ years.
2. By 4 to 4½ years, the majority of the urban and industrial children indicate pattern of copying, a triangle but the rural children do not to so. However, in the industrial group the majority of children do not show predominant or complete patterns.
3. The majority of the urban children arrive at a uniform pattern of copying in terms of direction of drawing by 4½ years. That is, they draw the sides of the triangle from the apex to the base and base from left to right. None of the rural groups show this pattern where as in the industrial group it is shown only by the children of Calcutta.
4. The majority of the urban children are able to make at least too well designed concerns by 4½ and 5 years. This ability is not seen in the majority of the rural and industrial children. The exceptions are the rural boys of Calcutta and industrial children of Calcutta, Hyderabad and Madras who show this ability by 4½ to 5 years.
5. Only the urban and industrial children of Calcutta found to make a well balance triangle. No other group is found to be able to do it. The urban children and the industrial boys of Calcutta can do it from 4 years where industrial girls do it at 5 years.

Colour

1. The urban boys from the majority of the centres name black by 3 years, red by 2½ to 3½ years, yellow and white by 4½ to 5 years. The urban girls from the majority of the centres name black by 2½ to 3 years, red by 3 to 3½ years, white by 4 years, green and yellow by 4½ years and blue by 4½ to 5 years.

2. The rural boys and girls from the majority of the centres name black by 4 to 5 years and red by 4½ to 5 years. While the rural boys name white at 5 years the rural girls do it by 4 to 4½ years.
3. The industrial boys from the majority of the centres name black by 3 to 4 years, red by 3½ to 4 years and white by 4 to 5 years. The industrial girls from the majority of the centres name black by 3½ to 4 years, white by 4 to 4½ years and red by 4½ to 5 years.
4. The majority of the industrial boys and girls are not able to name blue, green and yellow.
5. In the urban and rural areas, girls tend to name the colour a little earlier than the girls but the industrial children from the majority of the centres do not show any such difference.

This study undertaken on a nation wide scale to obtained developmental norms of Indian children. This perhaps the only study available for research worker. The results are quite useful in developmental diagnosis of pre-school children. The methodology and statistical techniques used are reasonably sound.

Butter and Jung (1970) investigated the developmental effect of sensory modality on form recognition in children. The subjects were 144 children from the kindergarten, first, second and third grades of elementary schools located in semi rural communities. The subjects were presented with a randomized sequence of 20 different three-dimensional forms. Each subject could see, or feel or see and feel the forms while trying to locate a matching cutout visually on a form board containing 50 cutouts of varying size, shape and orientation. Each form was available for 15 second after which subject made a response. Analysis of variance indicated a significant main effect of modality and of age. A moderate modality age interaction trend was also evident. As a consequence, the change with age in the relative efficiency of haptic versus bimodal performance was reported. A test of the simple effect of age on bimodal performance yielded an F ratio which barely missed significance. This study has shown that haptic performance improves gradually in kindergarten and third grade children. Visual performance stabilizes by about 5½ years of age. The capacity to integrate bimodal information undergoes important changes even at a latter age.

Harris, Schaller and Milter (1970) conducted a study on the effects of stimulus type on performance in a colour-form sorting task with pre-school, kindergarten, first grade and third-grade children. The sample consisted of 100 children, 50 boys and 50 girls ranging from pre-schoolers to third grade judged which of the two silhoelttes was "more like" a third, that was indeed with one figure in colour, to the other in shape. Each 'S' 24 with "Scrambled" figures, 24 with geometric figures. Across age groups, from matches were most frequent figures. The difference were however small. The number of "form preferences" and "strength" of preference increased significantly with age, but at all ages form matches predominated. There were no sex differences. Performance on trials 1-3 correlated highly with performance on trials 4-72.

Walter and Women (1971) conducted a study on the naming of primary colours by children and the results showed that the ability of girls to identify primary colours by name is greater than that of boys.

Bond (1972) conducted a study on perception of form by the human infant. In this study the young infant's responses to visual patterns is examined, with an emphasis on what these responses indicate about the capacity of form perception in the infant. Both visual scanning patterns and discrimination data were treated. The main conclusion was that the perception of the infant is qualitatively similar to that of the adults.

The relationship between colour naming and colour recognition abilities of pre-school children were investigated by Kimbal and Dale (1972). They tested the effect of memory, language on memory using 3, 4 year old children. The results indicated that their ability to name and recognition accuracy was significantly related to the children's ability to name colours. However chronological age, mental age I.Q. were significant confounding factors in the relationship between naming ability and used recognition accuracy. There was a significant tendency on the part of all the children to use their own colour names.

Belmont (1972) studied the relation of age and intelligence to short-term, colour memory. The study tested the relation of age or I.Q. effects to short-term forgetting rate. In order to overcome problems of differential task difficulty for different ages or I.Q. levels of each subject was pretested to determine the number of colours that he could recall first short perfectly at a Osec interval. All subjects were then given 4-, 8-, and 12s and filled and unfilled intervals using the number of colours determined in the pre-test. The results showed that the number of colours recalled was found to decrease with increasing intervals, and filled intervals. There was no interaction of age or I.Q. by type of interval. It was concluded that age and I.Q. have strong influences on acquisition, and retrival, but the forgetting rate is independent of this subject variables.

Lowee (1973) conducted a study on a developmental study of part-whole relations in visual perception. The subjects were 5–9 years old children. They were matched the shape of (a) small squares embedded in large rectangles and (b) small rectangles embedded in large squares. Predictions made were that (a) the influence of the whole on the perception of the point would be greater at the 5 years old level and (o) this effect of the whole made the points look to the child some what like the whole figure of which the point is a number. Both predictions were supported by the data. The results showed that five year old perceived the small squares as more rectangular, and the small rectangles as more square like; significantly more than the older age groups, each result representing a shift towards the shape of the whole configuration.

Stein and Mandler (1974) investigated the development of detection and recognition of orientation of geometric and real figures. The subjects were black and white kindergarten and second-grade children. They were tested for the accuracy of detection and recognition of orientation and location changes in pictures of real world and geometric figures. No differences were found in the accuracy of recognition between two kinds of pictures, but patterns of verbalization differed on specific transformations. Differences were also found between kindergarten and second grade on an initial recognition task. Practice or a matching-to-sample task, eliminated differences on a second recognition task. Few ethnic differences were found on accuracy of recognition, but significant differences were found in amount of verbal output as specific transformations. For both groups mention of orientation changes were marked reduced when location changes were percent.

Farnham Diggory and Gregg (1975) made on the attempt to study the colour form and function as dimensions of natural classification, reaction time and response strategies. They studied the behaviour of 5 years old and adults and measured in a matching to sample task using pictures of familiar objects and events. Subjects were matched on properties of colour form and function or compounds of these cues. On the basis of reaction times and age movements, inferences could be made about the subjects classification; process which were executed as efficiency by 5 years old as by the adults. Results showed other process which showed developmental differences. For properties, while difficult for children to extract, appeared to be utilised by them in the classification of familiar objects even though other properties were available.

Brittain (1976) made an attempt to study the effect of background shape on the ability of children to copy geometric forms. Children can normally be expected to copy a circle at 3, a square at 4, and a triangle at 5 years of age on standard 8½" x 11" paper. This study hypothesized that the shape of the background paper influences these norms. Fifty three nursery school children copied each of these geometric forms on various shaped background paper. The main findings of the study are as follows. Copying was easiest when the figure and the shape of the background paper had identical forms. Among the three figures chosen the circle was easiest, triangle was the most difficult. A very important question has been raised namely that the children who were copying the figure are substantially influenced by the shape of the background supplied. Therefore it is not very accurate to merely say the child can copy of figure without reference to the back-ground supplied. Therefore it is not very accurate to merely say the child can copy of figure without reference to the background. The author has finally concluded that the usual developmental sequence of circle-square-triangle, may be partially an artefact of typical four-sided rectangular or a square background of the paper.

Melkman, Koriat and Pardo (1976) studied the preferences for colour and form in pre-schoolers as related to colour and form differentiation. The preference for colour or form as a basis for similarity judgements among pre-schoolers (age 2–5) and its relationship to the differentiation of colour and form concepts as indexed by discrimination, identification and labelling were investigated. The hypo-thesis that an early stage form preference is present was confirmed. This was followed by the colour preference and a subsequent shift to form preference. That relative salience a dimension, develops in parallel to its relative degree of differentiation was not supported.

Christine and Richard (1976) studied visual dimensional dominance, and haptic form recognition. They selected 82 preschoolers for dimensional dominance by asking them to make similarities judgements about 2 dimensional geometric figures varying in form, colour and size. Subjects participated in two sets of haptic form recognition of 3 dimensional forms once with one hand and ones with two hands. The results showed that the recognition performance of form dominant Ss, form was substantially superior to be performance of non-form Ss. Ss of mixed dominance improved on the second test, generality as significant type of dominance tests inter-action. Order of administration of dominance and haptic tests had no significant influence on recognition performance.

Northman and Black (1976) studied as examination of errors in children visual and haptic-tactual memory for random forms. They selected 48 children 12 boys and 12 girls from each of grades 1 and 3. They were given a memory task for recognition of random Polygons of 4, 8, 12, 16 and 20 sides, these forms were presented either visually or haptically. The results showed that visual memory was superior to haptic memory and performance on both tasks improved with age, analysis of error-type and sideness, the two variables of a prior interest indicated. The curvilinear relationship between errors and sideness suggested difficult in identifying shapes of intermediate complexity.

Kalyani Devi (1979) studied the colour naming and colour recognition abilities of pre-scholars. The total sample for this study were 120 children. Both boys and girls were included in this study. Total sample was divided into two groups. (a) Experimental group and (b) control group. The sample belonged to the age groups of 2½ to 3½, 3½ to 4½ and 4½. to 5½ years. The investigator used both primary and secondary colours for the study. Each child was individually tested. The test was conducted in two sessions. First one was the naming task and the second one was the recognition task. The investigator asked the children to name both the primary and secondary colours one by one. After naming task the child was given recognition task. In experimental group test items were presented on one day, on the third day the items were again presented. Retest was given after 10 days. At that time other materials were also used (Ribbons & Bangles). The results indicated that, as the age increased the colour naming and recognition abilities did not increase. There was no differences between boys and girls in colour naming and recognition, abilities. There was differences between different schools depending upon the experiences and opportunities given who has its effect on colour naming and colour recognition abilities of children.

Garner (1980) investigated the form and function information in young children's concepts of familiar objects. The sample consisted of 16 first grade subjects, 16 second grade subjects and 16 third grade subjects. The relative contribution of form and function information to concepts of 10 objects were investigated. Children were asked to generate information about what objects look like and what people do with the objects in interviews with the investigator. The results showed that there was a significant difference between grade level and response type interaction. For first grades, function information about objects took precedence. For second graders on the other hand, form information took precedence. Form information responses were further analysed by particular type (e.g. shape, size) and all responses were surveyed for any description offered only once by any subject.

The role of symmetry in infant form discrimination was studied by Fisher, Ferdinandsen and Bornstein (1981). The study examined whether infants can discriminate form on the basis of symmetrical organisation when other stimulus factors were tested in a habituation-dishabituation, discrimination Parading using vertically symmetrical, horizontally ones. This pattern of results suggested that the global organization embodied, in vertical symmetry promotes perceptual discrimination. Twelve additional four months old were habituated and tested with 2 vertical patterns. Their failure to demonstrate a reliable patterns of distribution suggests that babies respond to goodness of organisation rather than to details unique to particular symmetrical patterns.

What emerges from a review of some of the studies on perceptual development in children, is the fact that form discrimination is present even among infants as early as at six months, and there is a cyclical variation in the relative salience of colour and form in subsequent years of childhood. There appears to be no satisfactory explanation as to, why form is more potent than colour in early years of life. It is also not clear whether such a Phenomena is universally observable among children across different cultural environments. There is a controversy with reference to form and colour discrimination. It is possible that such a prepotency and cyclical shift in the salience of the colour and form has some biological adaptive value. In such a case environmental factors have to be also invoked to find answers to the questions.

NIPCCD (1984) conducted a study to assess the impact of pre-school programme on the beneficiaries of the ICDS scheme. Ten tests were used to assess the children on various aspects of cognitive development like sequential thinking test, time perception test, shape discrimination test, colour discrimination test and Draw-a-Man Test. Significant differences were found in the abilities of naming, identifying and matching the shapes and colours. The test scores of beneficiary group have emerged to be consistently higher than that of the non-beneficiary group.

A study carried out by Ammani Devi (1984) on the effect of enriched perceptual experiences through selected books on the performances of pre-school children on simple perceptual tasks revealed that the environment of perceptual experiences increased perceptual ability, decreased the time taken for having the colour verbally and significantly reduces the possible errors in the colours naming task. There was a significant difference in perceptual discrimination task of colour, form and also under haptic condition with the enriched experiences. Significant sex differences were also noticed on colour naming task, perceptual discrimination of colour and form separately and in haptic discriminating tasks.

Patrica, Victor and Stephen (1987) assessed the performance of 4 and 5 years old on geometric analogy tasks. Each task consisted of 16 analogy problems that were presented in a manipulative, game like context and that used attribute blocks that varied on the dimensions of colour, size and shape.

Experiment, demonstrated that many of the pre-schoolers were capable of applying analogical reasoning in the selection of geometric analogy problems of the form A, B and C. It is also found that children who did not consistently reason analogically showed evidence of a reasoning strategy that was governed by hierarchical rule structure.

Experiment 2 in which a modified version of the geometric analogy task in experiment 1 was used, confirmed the findings of the initial experiment with regard to the analogical reasoning ability of 4 years and 5 years old. The rule structure was verified for generally exhibited no consistent pattern, in their response errors.

Nurjahan (1994) studied the cognitive and language abilities of the pre-school children over a sample of 65 children, randomly selected from where school-going and non-school going children were available. Four school going children and twenty five non-school going children were selected randomly, from given anganwadies and five other different areas of Tirupati town. The age group of these children was 3.0 to 6.0 years. The cognitive and language ability tests developed by Children's Media Laboratory, NCERT were adopted. Results revealed that significant differences were found between school-going and non-school going children with regard to form and colour discrimination tests. Significant age difference was found.

Suman and Indra's (1996) study focused on the level of concept formation in pre-school children from three different categories of schools in Chandigarh. Sample consisting of 124 Ss from different schools, ranging between the age groups of 3½ to 5 years were matched on age, sex and socio-economic status. The final sample consisted of 60 children, 30 boys and 30 girls, who were then administered five concept formation tasks namely: Shape, size, colour, number and seriation to study the level of concept formation in pre-school children, from three different categories of schools. Interview was conducted on teachers teaching these pre-school children to know about the quality of educational experiences being provided in the schools. Results showed that Ss from the Laboratory school performed better than those from Government and Private schools on concept formation tasks. No significant differences were observed in the level of concept formation.

Aruna and Kalyani Devi (1996) studied the cognitive abilities of pre-school children in Laboratory and Private Nursery Schools over a sample of 92 children belonging to two age groups 3.7 to 4.0 and 4.0 to 4.6 years of Laboratory and Private Nursery Schools. The cognitive ability tests developed by NCERT were used to study the cognitive abilities of children. Results showed the significant differences between Laboratory and Private Nursery School children in object vocabulary, listening comprehension, acquaintance with environment, shape and colour discrimination. Significant age trends were observed and no sex differences were found in both the schools.

B. Studies on the specific effects of environmental variables and prolonged deprivation on the performance of children on perceptual tasks.

In recent times there is an enormous increase in the research studied on disadvantaged children. The main focus of most of the studies is on the cognitive functioning in relation to socio-cultural environment of children. The following is a brief review of some of the most important reported studies in this area. It is not the intention to extensively cover the literature, but to highlight such studies which has investigated the specific effects of environmental variables and prolonged deprivation on the performance of children on perceptual tasks.

Motivational aspects of changes in I.Q. test performance of culturally deprived nursery school children were studied by Zingler and Butterfield (1968). The children were selected from 2 nursery schools. Thirty five children were taken from attending nursery schools and 19 children were selected who are not attending nursery schools. Two categories of children were belonged to lower class homes. Intelligence testing procedures allowing the separation of motivational from cognitive achievement determinants of changes in standard Binnet IQs were employed. The children who attend nursery school increased significantly more in their IQ scores (Standard administration) from the beginning to the end of the nursery school year than did the children who did not attend nursery school. The findings indicated that the increase in IQ which resulted from the nursery school experience was due to the reduction in the effects of debilitating motivational factors rather than to changes in rate of intellectual development.

Olmsted and Sigel (1970) studied the generality of colour-form preference as a function of materials and task requirement among lower class Negro children. The author investigated the generality of colour-form performance by administering several colour-form tasks to the same group of subjects. These tasks employed geometrics, familiar objects, and pictures of these objects as stimuli, and sorting, categorizing, and matching to standard as procedures. It was hypothesized that preferences for individual subjects would be task specific. The subjects selected for this study were 41 lower class black boys, and 34 girls, ranging in age from 61 to 76 months, with a mean age of 68.3 months. The results indicated that the predominant made of response varied with the task employed. Colour-form preferences vary with age. Sex and school yielded no significant differences.

The adverse effect of socially disadvantaged condition on intellectual development in Indian children is confirmed by (Singh 1977). There is however a controversy as to the exact basis for such adverse effect arising from exclusively poor environment. Jensen argues (1972) that inferior intellectual facility of socially disadvantaged children is contributed by inferior genetic basis. There are others who disagree with jensen and attribute to poor quality of perceptual experience.

Benergi and Muralidharan (1974) conducted a study to discuss the effect of pre-school education on the language and intellectual development of underprivileged children. The experimental group was formed from kindergarten class of a good nursery school who had 2 years of pre-schooling. The control group was formed from class I of a primary school who had not attended any pre-school. A suitable story was narrated to the children individually and the responses of the children were taken to measure their language development. Phatak's Draw-a-man test was used to measure the intellectual development. The results showed that the children in the pre-school are consistently better than the primary school children in all aspects of language and intellectual development. The pre-school age was found to be at advantage in both language and intellectual development in spite of the fact they were chronologically younger than the primary school group and were still in the kindergarten class.

Casey (1979) studied the colour versus form discrimination learning in three years old children of different socio-economic groups. The results indicated high socio-economic children have more opportunities to develop their colour and form concepts whereas the low socio-economic children have less opportunities to develop these tasks.

Mumbauer and Miller (1980) studied the socio economic background as related to cognitive functioning in pre-school children. Thirty two advantaged and thirty two disadvantaged children were selected for the study. They were administered a battery of tests including measures of general intellectual functioning learning performance, impulsivity reflectivity, ability to inhibit motor behaviour upon request, and object exploratory behaviour. The results supported the hypothesis that culturally disadvantaged preschool children are efficient in intellectual performance than advantaged children of the same age. Only tentative support was found for the hypothesis, that disadvantaged Ss are more impulsive in response disposition. The data did not support the hypothesis that the culturally disadvantaged children inhibit their motor responses less upon verbal request or manifest less object curiosity than the advantaged children.

Comparing 300 socially disadvantaged with an equal number of advantaged school children in Andhra Pradesh, Ushasri (1980) reported no difference in the mental abilities of children in the two groups. This particular finding is at deviance from the previous reports. Since the author has not reported the criteria of children classifying the socially disadvantaged children except the fact that they are all children enrolled in schools it is difficult to comment. Even the author does not attempt to explain the fact that the two groups of children did not show any difference between intelligence test scores.

Puspa (1980) conducted a study on social deprivation and cognitive development of primary school children, in order to find the association or impact of social deprivation on cognitive abilities and cognitive styles of children. She took the children from advantaged and dis-advantaged backgrounds by selecting children from different types of schools or for example Government aided schools, and children from semi-urban, rural and tribal environments. The sample consisted of 265 (210 advantaged and 55 disadvantaged) children from I, III and IV grades in the age range of 5–12 years. To measure social deprivation, prolonged deprivation scale (PDS) developed by Misra and Tripathi (1978) was adapted. To measure the cognitive styles she used Draw A person test (D.A.P.) and children's Embedded Figure Test (CEFT) tests were used. To measure the cognitive abilities W.I.S.C. namely picture completion, kohs blocks design and object assembly were choosen. The findings of the study are that social deprivation has significant retarding cosequences for cognitive functioning. It was found that deprivation experienced by the individual in various areas of life restricts the growth of cognitive styles and abilities. In all the test scores the significant correlations indicated that higher the deprivation higher the field dependence in children. The association between social deprivation and cognitive domain was highly significant. She also found that the adverse effect of physical, cultural and parental deprivation on the cognitive development of the children.

Kagan, Finely, Rogoff and Elizabeth (1980) made a cross cultural study of cognitive development in the children from three communities. The sample approximately had equal number of boys and girls. In Cambridge sample was composed of 59 children. They are middle class children and their parents were educated. In San pedro 126 children were selected. These children were selected on the basis of their parents occupation. In San Marks 140 subjects were selected (6–13 years). Each child was tested individually. Each testing session was approximately 15–40 minutes long and the number of test sessions were 4 to 12. The tests consisted of classification test, memory span for pictures, memory for pictures with operations, memory span for orientation of dolls, memory span for doll operation, memory span for words and conservation of matter. The results were as follows:

For memory span test, a significant differences among the three settings and ages occurred for all three span tests. Sex differences were rare. Since the increments in performance with age appeared continuous, no internal comparisons between adjacent ages were made.

In all the memory tests, Cambridge children displayed the best performance, followed by San Pedro and than San Markas. San Marcas children showed their greatest improvement between 10 and 11 years of age, San Pedro between ages 9 and 10, Cambridge between ages 7 & 8.

In doll span test the analysis of variance yielded a significant effect of culture, with Cambridge children performing best followed by Sanpedro and then San Macros; as well as increasing age effect across all cultures and within each culture. San Macras children showed their greatest improvement between 11 and 12 years of age, San Pedro between 9 and 10 years, Cambridge between 7 and 8 years.

In word span test analysis of variance again yielded a significant effect for culture, with Cambridge children performing than San Pedro and San Pedro better than San Macras Children. Performance increase with age across groups as well as within each of the three cultures.

The San Macras children showed their greatest improvement between 7 & 8 years of age, earlier than on the picture and doll procedures. Sanpedro and Cambridge children improved most between 9 & 10 years of age. Of the three span tests, the Indian children of all ages found the dolls most difficult because we suggest, the unit of information to be memorized was least familiar to them and because the doll task involved interference among the information in the adjacent items. The Cambridge children may have been utilising more effective strategies to reduce interference on all tasks.

Cognitive abilities of pre-school children is studied by Sudha Rani (1987). This study cosisting of 27 boys and 33 girls of both urban and rural backgrounds attending Anganwadis in and around Tirupati were given the cognitive tests. The study concluded that there are significant differences in the cognitive abilities of urban and rural children.The overall scoring of the urban children is about 10 per cent higher than those of the rural background. No sex difference was found. The superiority of the urban children over their rural counterparts can be attributed to environmental stimulation.

Lavanya (1994) investigated the cognitive and language abilities of pre school children in Piler, Chittoor district. A sample of 30 high and 30 law income groups of 3.0 to 4.5 years and 4.5 to 6.0 were randomly selected from 3 anganwadis and 3 private schools. From the total sample, 32 boys and 28 girls were selected from both economic groups. The tests developed by NCERT were adopted.

Analysis revealed significant differences between high and low economic groups and no sex difference was found.

Cognitive and language abilities of Hindus and Scheduled Tribe children of 3.0 to 6.0 years was studied by Karuna Kumari (1994). In Hindus 40 boys and 40 girls (40 + 40 = 80) and in Scheduled Tribes 13 boys and 13 girls (13 + 13 = 26) were selected randomly from the anganwadis where both the groups were enrolled. The tests developed by NCERT were used. it was found that Hindu children were performed high in colour and form discrimination tests than Scheduled Tribe children.

Fathima and Zeheda (1994) undertaken a study on the concept formation among pre-school children with reference to age, gender, and economic status. A total sample of 200 children were drawn by simple random sampling procedure, selected equally from high and low economic status. Equal number of 80 boys and 80 girls were from age groups 3–3½ years and 4–4½ years respectively and 20 boys and 20 girls of 5 years self-constructed tools were used to assess the formation of concepts viz., concept of colour, time, number, size and shape in young children. Analysis of the results by application of 'F' and 't' revealed that there was significant difference in the formation of concept of colour, time, number, size and shape between the three age groups. But no significant differences were observed between boys and girls with respect to concept of colour, time, size and shape between the three age groups. But no significant differences were observed between boys and girls with respect to concept of colour, time, and size whereas, significant results existed with regard to concept of number and shape. Economic status was found to influence the formation of diffeence concepts.

Two studies on mental development, intersensory integration in children who are survivors of malnutrition can be sited from the available literature to support the evidence the malnutrition causes damages to cognitive abilities.

A classic study by Cravioto, Delicardie, Pinero, Lindoro, Arroyo and Alcade (1971) investigated neuro integrative development in school children recovered from malnutrition. Thirty nine children who were earlier refer to pediatrics unit in army hospital in Mexico city with severe malnutrition when they are 4 to 30 months old constituted the sample. These children assessed by trained psychologist using WISC. Auditory-visual, visual-kinesthetic integration were evaluated using a special procedure developed by Birch Belmont (1969), Birch and Leffort (1963). The results indicated that the distribution of intelligence scores markedly showed with a large number of subjects scoring in the lower range of values. When the respective performance of the siblings and the malnourished groups are compared it becomes evident that the children who were severely malnourished are significantly over-represented in the lower extreme. If the verbal and performance scales of the intelligence was noticed that significantly lower scores are attained by the previously malnourished children in tasks requiring verbal elements as well as in tasks demanding non-verbal responses. Both with regard to Audio-visual integration and visual-kinesthetic integration, the performance of previously malnourished children was significantly inferior to the performance of their siblings. The authors are cautions in generalizing the findings as sufficient proof, in support of malnutrition directly affecting central nervous system is not available. Social and familial environment as casative factors can not be totally excluded from a proper consideration of the phenomenon.

Das and Priyani (1980) studied the late effects of malnutrition on cognitive competence. They investigated whether an episode of malnutrition, leading to hosplitalization, further depressed the intellectual performance of children from the disadvantaged economic and social class. Children of Colombo, Srilanka, who had been hospitalised for marasmus and Kwashiarker were traced and compared on tests of cognitive functions with a groups of children from their neighbourhood, matched on age and sex.They selected 42 patients and 42 controls were studied. Thirty three siblings of the patients were also compared with another group of 33 age and sex matched neighbourhood children. Results showed little difference between the groups on tests of cognitive functions (eg. figure copying, Digit span, & colour naming) and a strong relationship between the childs years of attendence at school at the cognitive tests. It is concluded that an episode of severe malnutrition does no more than cronic undernutritiion does to disadvantaged children.

Some Comments

From the foregoing review of reported studies the following salient observations may be recorded;

1. The perceptual development in children takes place in an orderly sequence from infancy onwards.
2. There is a cyclical shift in the salience of form and colour in perceptual discrimination.
3. Sex differences are not reported.
4. Perceptual experience and cognitive functioning are intimately related to environmental variables.
5. Disadvantaged children (children who are exposed to poor quality of perceptual experience) consistently perform inferior to advantaged children on cognitive functions.

The dynamic interaction between the environment and the growth related functions are not yet clear. All that the studies so far have established is the harmful effects of deprivation on the development of children. Beyond this no one has foregod ahead to explain the pathways to this end state in clear terms. One can pointout certain constraints in integrating the findings of diverse studies. For example, the definition of disadvantaged condition is not uniformly consistent across several studies. It is needless to state that the term disadvantage is a relative term, a natural disadvantage in one environment, may not be so in another environment. Therefore comparing the performance aross different environments is difficult, and is influenced by artefacts. It is particularly shown, that when the performance is assessed by tests, which are themselves heavily loaded with an environmetal bias the results are confirmed. It is necessry, therefore to introduce some methodological refinements, in a proper evaluation of the effects of the environment on growth related functions. It may be more partinent to ask; relative to one's own environment, how well the child is effecient in assimilation and utilisation of informaiton. probably the confusion that one sees, in the literature on environment (Social disadvantage) and mental development may be attributed to lack of clear definition of the terms and inappropriate use of tools. These comments are made as general observations, thoug they are not directly related to our research interest.

It may be also seen from the literature, that research studies focussing on cross cultural comparisons, are not as many as they ought to be. Though in India nearly 40% of the total population are children, and majority of them are growing up in a relatively deprived conditions, the research data are depressingly meagre. It is against this background that the present research investigation was planned. The intention was to scientifically gather evidence on perceptual discrimination (Form and colour) among preschool children in relation to the specific influence of the condition of the prolonged deprivation.

3

Statement of the Problem and Hypotheses

Justification

A critical study of reported literature on perceptual development in children reveals, that a growing child, a whatever environment it is growing, interprets the sensory-motor experiences, in an increasingly complex manner. The development takes place in an orderly sequence, and that this order and sequence are likely to be disturbed due to anomalies in environment, as well as the internal conditions of the child. Acquisition of perceptual constancies are not only necessary but or vital to perceive patterns of sensory stimulations.

Perception of form and colour is fundamental to perceptual experience. In every day world, objects exist in both these dimensions. The ability to discriminate objects both in form and colour involves cognitive functions, whose mechanism is not thoroughly understood. For example, the colour form salience in visual interpretation and the cyclical shift in the potency of form and colour during the growth period are not reasonably understood. The impact of environment and the pathways to the interaction of environment with the child's sensory-motor experience is subjected to research only in the recent times. Sophisticated tools to quantify the environment have been developed only recently. Therefore it is necessary to have more scientific information on the performance of children on perceptual task across different cultural samples. The available data is not adequate to offer a neat explanation for several issues concerning the perceptual development in children, particularly in relation to socio-cultural environment.

A proper scientific definition of the term, environment and the environmental deprivation, is a first step. The term deprivation is vague and relative, and therefore the essential components have to be defined in clear terms. Environment includes both physical and non-physical stimuli available in the immediate surroundings in which the child lives and grows. A good definition should account for the complexity of experiences, a child under goes and the quality of experience which is not uniformly same for all the children. As a matter of fact that socio-cultural environment is to be regarded, as a continuum, at one end of which are those whose biological and other needs are fulfilled satisfactorily, while at the opposite end are those who struggle and fight to fulfil the very same needs and fail to attain a reasonable fulfilment of the needs. Viewed from this aspect both environment and deprivation are global concepts, involving innumerable empirical referents and experiences very important to human life. There is another aspect to the concept of deprivation namely prolonged exposure to conditions of deprivation, generation after generation. A vicious circle is sure to develop and produce a progressive decline in the growth related functions.

The main tennets of the present research problem reflect the theoretical arguments presented above and the practical necessity to understand the perceptual experience of children in their early childhood. Preschool education is intended to provide opportunity for children to have better experience which form a base for healthy growth and development. It is complementary to home experience, and covers up whatever deficiencies that may be present in the homes of children. We need information about the fundamentals of perceptual deficiencies of children in designing appropriate sensory-motor experiences to children. Therefore the present research was planned to study the influence of some basic demographic variables and prolonged deprivation as it exists in the sociocultural environment, on the performance of preschool children on a task requiring form and colour discrimination. It is intended to assess qualitatively and quantitatively the errors in the performance under various experimental conditions of form-colour discrimination.

The following hypotheses were set up for empirical verification, based on the review of extant literature presented in the previous chapter.

In the multivariate analysis the five independent variables are namely *Age, Sex, quality of school environment, deprivation level* and type of perceptual task, and the dependent variable is percent errors in discrimination. The hypotheses in terms of the result to be expected are;

1. Both form and colour discrimination improves with age.

    i) The main effect due to age is significant.

2. Boys and girls do not significantly differ between themselves in their performance on perceptual tasks.

    ii) The main effect due to sex is not significant.

3. Better the level of quality of environment of the school, better is the performance on the form colour discrimination task.

    i) The main effect due to level of quality of environment of the school is significant.

4. The performance of children on form colour discrimination tasks who are relatively more deprived, is inferior to the performance of children who are less deprived.

    i) The main effect due to deprivation level is significant.

    Note :Performance, under the condition, in which the child has to sort plastic cutout figures of different forms disregarding their colour is more difficult than simple sorting based on form only. Similarly sorting plastic cutout figures according to their colour disregarding form is more difficult, than sorting the same plastic cutout figures based on the form only. Absence of visual cue makes their task of form discrimination more difficult when the child has to differed upon haptic experience.

The exact procedure of collecting experimental data and statistical treatment of data obtained are chosen to highlight the above hypotheses.

Method and Procedure

General Plan

The purpose of the research study is to experimentally evaluate the effects of age, sex and prolonged depravation on perceptual discrimination. It is proposed to study the performances of preschool age children on perceptual discrimination tasks under different experimental conditions.

The research study therefore involves two stages. In the first stage preliminary evaluation of the major tools to be employed has to be considered. The second stage concern's the measurement of performance of children on perceptual discrimination tasks under previously designed experimental conditions.

The sample of children in three age groups namely 3^+, 4^+, 5^+ years is to be drawn from a population of children enrolled in nursery/kindergarten/balwadies both in Tirupati town and near by villages with in a radius of about 6 to 10 kilometers. It is propose to have equal number of boys and girls in the sample to facilitate easy statistical analysis.

The deprivation is propose to be measured using the prolonged deprivation scale (PDS) developed by Misra and Tripathi (1978) with suitable modifications to suit the local conditions. In addition the quality of the environment of the schools in which the children are attending is also proposed to be quantitatively evaluated by developing a special scale for the purpose. This is to be called preschool evaluation scale (PES).

The perceptual discrimination tasks are designed to measure the child's ability to discriminate three common forms like a square, a triangle and a circle. Colour is added as an additional variable. It is proposed to test the child's ability to discriminate colours together with the forms of objects by appropriately designing the experimental conditions of the administration of the discrimination tasks. Three colours are chosen namely red, green and yellow. It is planned to test the perceptual discrimination by asking the child to sort from a pool of plastic cutout figures of different forms and colours. Three different conditions are chosen. They are;

1. Sorting plastic cutout figures (all of same colour) on the basis of their form only (Form sorting only).
2. Sorting plastic cut out figures of different colours and forms into their respective *forms* dis-regarding their colours (Form sorting only).
3. Sorting plastic cutout figures of different forms and colours into their respective colours (disregarding their forms)
4. Sorting plastic cutout figures of different forms and colours into their respective form and cutout both being identical.
5. Identifying the forms by touch without the aid of visual cues (haptic).

The relevant controls such as the number of cutout figures to be sorted the size of cutout figures and others sources likely to influence validity of the data will be applied to the experimental procedure. To assess the possible influence of intellectual ability on the performance, a suitable test of mental ability like a Draw-A-person Test is proposed to be used.

It is planned to compare the performance of children on the perceptual tasks by recording the errors under each conditions of the experiment and comparing them between the children of different age groups, sexes, levels of deprivation and different levels of quality of environment. For this purpose two levels of derivations are setup and operationally defined. Similarly the quality of environment is also expressed in three levels, again operationally defined. It is proposed to subject the data to a multivariate analysis in which the independent effects of age, sex, prolonged deprivation and quality of school environment on the dependent variables namely the percent errors under the different conditions of the experiment are tested. The results of the analysis will be interpreted in the light of the review of relevant literature, and the hypotheses set up.

Subjects for the First Stage of the Study

Eighteen boys and 18 girls were selected from three school of three defined levels of quality of environment. There were 12 children in each level (6 boys and 6 girls). With reference to the age, there were 2 boys and 2 girls at each age. This is replicated across the three levels of the quality of environment (2 × 2 × 3 × 3 = 36).

Subjects for the Second Stage of Study

A total of 156 children, 78 boys and 78 girls were selected at random from 13 preschools in and around Tirupati town. At each age of the three age groups there were 26 boys and 26 girls (26 +26) × 3 = 156. With regard to the three levels of quality of environment the number of children varied. In level C_1 there were 12 (6 boys and 6 girls), (6 × 2 12). In level C_2 there were 96 children (48 boys and 48 girls) (48 × 2 =96). In level C3 there were 48, (24 boys and 24 girls) (24 × 2 = 48). (12 + 96 + 48 = 156).

Tools and Materials of Research

Tools and Materials used in the present research study are as follows :

1. A tool to evaluate the quality of environment of the preschools (PES).
2. A tool to evaluate the prolonged deprivation scale (PDS).
3. Draw-A -person test.
4. Materials for testing perceptual discrimination

Pre-school Evaluation Scales (PES)

Description

The scale consists of four components of the environment—Physical, human, and activity and programmes. The components includes are,

a) Physical setting
b) Staff
c) Equipment
d) Programmes

Under each component relevant items are listed so as to form a scale ranging between *optimal or good* and *poor* with regard to their quality. Each item is scored according to the scheme in which 3 points are given for optimal, 2 points are given for moderate, 1 point is given for poor.

Method of Administration

The investigator evaluated the preschool with the help of the scale by personally visiting and observing the school in an informal fashion. Care was taken to see that the concerned people in the school were not given the impression that the school is being evaluated, which would avoid prejudicing them to boost the rating.

As mentioned earlier point scale scoring system was adopted. Each item of the scale was assigned a point credit according to the degree of quality previously defined. The total number of credits possible is 30. An arbitrary scale of the quality of environment was developed. Three levels namely C_1, C_2, and C_3 are designated if the scores range between 20–30, 20 and below 10 respectively. Higher the score greater the quality of the environment.

A Tool to Evaluate the Prolonged Deprivation Scale (PDS) (Modified Version)

The scale used in this study is a modified version of the original prolonged deprivation scale developed by Misra and Tripathi (1978).

Description

This modified version consists of 63 items distributed over 13 deprivation areas. Each item has 5 scaled responses scaled in the direction of deprivation. Table 4.1 gives the modified version.

The number of items in certain areas have been altered. In addition to altering the number, some items have been reworded for better clarity and relevance. Thirty three items were omitted

Table 4.1 : Deprivation Areas, Number of Items and Maximum Possible Score on PD

Sl. No.	Deprivation Area	Number of Items		Maximum score possible on the modified scale
		Original	Modified	
1.	Housing condition (H.C.)	6	6	30
2.	Home Environment (H.E.)	8	8	40
3.	Economic Sufficiency (E.S.)	7	7	35
4.	Food (F)	4	4	20
5.	Clothing (C)	4	4	20
6.	Formal Education Experiences (F.E.E.)	7	3	15
7.	Childhood Experiences (C.E.)	5	5	25
8.	Rearing Experience (R.E.)	7	5	25
9.	Interaction with Parents (I.P.)	6	3	15
10.	Motivational Experience (M.E.)	11	2	10
11.	Religious Experiences (R.E.)	4	2	10
12.	Travel and Recreation (T.R.)	3	4	20
13.	Socio-culural Experiences (S.C.E.)	9	10	50
14.	Parental Characteristics (P.C.)	7	–	–
15.	Emotional Experiences (E.E.)	8	–	–
	Total	**96**	**63**	**315**

in all. There were the items which were found to be not suitable for local conditions. A separate answer sheet was specially designed for easy scoring of the prolonged deprivation scale.

Administration

The test is administrated through a personal visit to the homes of children and interviewing the parents, in addition to physical observation of the home conditions. Each item is given a score 1-5 on the rating scale. The record sheet is so designed that it possible to mark, quickly the value of rating by simply encircling the number & corresponding to the rating assigned. Approximately 45 minutes will be sufficient to go through the PDS.

Scoring

The scores on any deprivation area is the total of all the ratings obtained by the items in that deprivation area. This total is entered in a box provided on the separate sheet. The score on the entire scale is the sum of all the subtotals in each deprivation area. The maximum score possible is 315 (5 × 63 = 315). The scale continuum-extends from least deprivation to most derivation with corresponding scale various 1–5. So, highest possible score for any items is 5.

A Note on the Original Scale

The authors have described the background, the rationale, standardization data and norms in the manual published by National Psychological Corporation. The authors have reported a consistently high reliability coefficients for all the three types of reliabilities reported namely, inter-rater reliability test-retest reliability, and split half reliability. The reliability coefficients ranged between .59 to 95. The scale was validated using four forms of validity coefficients. The validity coefficients have been reported to be consistently and satisfactorily high. The test was also factor analysed using principal component method, and two factors were extracted. These factors were labelled A and B. The factor A included areas like housing condition, home environment and economic sufficiency etc. Factor B included, child-hood experiences, interaction with parents, religious experiences etc. Factor A accounted 91.8% factor B accounted for 8.2% of the total variance. The authors have interpreted factor A as representing physioeconomic deprivation, factor B as experiential deprivation. The sample for developing norms consisted of 645 males between 15-25 years.

Draw–A–Person Test

The use of human figure drawing as a measure of intelligence is well established (Good enough), 1926, Harris 1963). Paramila Phatak (1966) has adopted the Draw-a man-test to Indian conditions. She has further- shown that the scale is valid and reliable to an acceptable level in its practical applications.

Administration and Scoring

The test was administered and scored according to instructions given in Phatak's (1966) manual. The scoring scale consists of 21 categories, in which each category is given a weighted credit. Maximum scores possible on the scale is 62.

Materials used for Perceptual Discrimination tasks

The materials consisted of several plastic cutouts of circles, squares and triangles, cut from a plastic sheet of .25 cms. thickness. The following are the dimensions of the cutout figures.

Circles 2.5 cms diameter

Square 2.5 cms x 2.5 cms

Triangle All the three sides equal and are 2.5 cms

These plastic cutouts were not all of the same colour. There were *white* circles, *white* squares and *white* triangles, green circles, green squares and green triangles, red circles, red squares and red triangles, and yellow circles, yellow squares and yellow triangles. (Table 4.2 gives the details).

Table 4.2 : Details of the Materials Used for Perceptual Discrimination Tasks

Plastic cutout figures	*Colours*				*Total*
	White	*Red*	*Green*	*Yellow*	
Circle	5	10	10	10	35
Square	5	10	10	10	35
Triangle	5	10	10	10	35
Total	**15**	**30**	**30**	**30**	**105**

Materials used for Testing Haptic Perceptual Discrimination:

A rectangular box with slits at both ends for haptic testing. Perceptual discrimination under the condition of visual cue being eliminated.

This consisted of a rectangular wooden box 22 × 8 × 15 cms. whose outer surface was covered by blue rexine cloth. The box had the following dimensions.

There were two slites at the nearest and the farthest end of the box. The slit of nearest end had the following dimensions 11 cms x 9 cms. At the farthest end was a semicircular slit with a radius of 8 cms.

Plastic Bowls

There were four plastic bowls (three small and one big). *None of these four bowls had the same colours as the plastic cutouts.* The colour of the bowls was light blue. A Stop watch and the Record Sheet.

Procedure

Preliminary Evaluation of Major Tools

It was found necessary to make a preliminary evaluation of the major tools as well as the procedure for testing perceptual discrimination tasks.

The preschool evaluation scale was used to determine the level of quality of environment of the schools. In all, there were 26 schools both in Tirupati Town and in the surrounding out-skirts. As described earlier, the total possible score on preschool evaluation scale is 30. It was operationally defined that a score between 20–30 would be designated C_1 level; score between 10–20 as C_2 level; and a score below 10 as C_3 level. Lower the score poorer the quality of environment. Accordingly C_1 is superior to C_2 and C_2 is superior to C_3 with regard to the quality of environment. Making use of this scheme, these schools were identified whether it was of C_1 C_2 or C_3 type.

For the purpose of preliminary evaluation one school from each of the three level was selected. Twelve children were randomly selected from each of these three schools to constitute the preliminary sample. There were 36 children. To this sample the perceptual discrimination task was given in order to test the instructions, timing of tasks, suitability of the experimental procedure, recording the data etc.

Person Test

This was administered each child and scored as per instruction given in the manual and described earlier in this chapter.

Perceptual Discrimination Tasks

The procedure for testing the perceptual discrimination, involved sorting of plastic cutout figure of different forms and of different colours, under different previously determined conditions of the experiment. It was necessary to determine the optimal time for each of the five conditions. It was discovered during preliminary testing that the following time limit for the five conditions was most appropriate :

1. Sorting plastic cutout figures (white) 60s
2. Sorting plastic cutout figures of different colours and forms *into their respective forms* disregarding their colours (Form sorting only) 300s
3. Sorting plastic cutout figures of different forms and colours *into their respective colours* disregarding their forms (colours) 300s
4. Sorting plastic cutout figures of different forms and colours *into their respective form* and colour 600s
5. Identifying the plastic cutout figures by touch without the aid of visual cue (haptic)

The procedure for testing perceptual discrimination under haptic condition employed was found to be quite satisfactory. Earlier it was thought blind folding was necessary but it was soon discovered that children felt uncomfortable and also it was not possible to eliminate completely. Hence a rectangular box was peeping devise such that the child could tactually experience the cutout figures inside the box and give the responses. This procedure was found to be satisfactory.

Prolonged Deprivation Scale

The investigator, visited the homes of 36 children to acquaint herself with the use of the prolonged deprivation scale. This experience was very helpful in modifying some of the items.

Experimental Procedure

From out of the 26 schools in the pool, 13 schools were selected on the basis of their scores to represent the three levels chosen on PES. Each school was identified with the previously defined the level of quality of environment. From each school, children between 3 to 5 years were selected so as to constitute sample of subjects. As described earlier the sample had equal number of boys and girls at each age. There were a total number of 156 children.

Each child was administered the perceptual discrimination task individually in their respective schools by previous arrangement with the school authorities. The following is the detailed description of the procedure employed :

A) Sorting Plastic Cutout Figures (White only)

The child was seated on the floor and it was presented with the plastic figures (all white only). The experimenter arranged three plastic cutout figures, circle, square and triangle in a row and asked the child to place all the plastic cutouts of the same form as is in the row. One above the other. There were 15 (five for each form). Sixty seconds were allowed. The experimenter recorded the errors by counting wrong placements. Any wrong placement is due to *form confusion.*

B) Sorting the Plastic Cutout Figures of Different Colours and Forms into their Respective Forms (Forms Sorting only)

In this condition of the experiment the child is presented the plastic cutout figures which consisted of circle squares and triangles having three different colours namely Red, Yellow and Green (see Table 4.2). The total number of plastic cutout figures were 90. These were put in the large bowl. Three bowls of identical colour and size were placed in front of the child and the child was asked to sort the plastic cutout figures into these bowls depending on their form only. The child is asked to disregard the colour. For example a *red* square and *green* square should be put in the same bowl but not a *red square* with the *green triangle.* Thus the three bowls, should have plastic cutout figures all of the same form. Three hundred seconds were allowed as a maximum time for this task. The experimenter recorded error namely *form confusion* (a square being put in the box containing triangle and so on). The experimenter also noted the total number of figures sorted out within the time limit. Since this number (the number sorted) may vary from subject to subject, it was thought the present error would be a better score and therefore the error score were expressed as percentages.

C) Sorting the Plastic Cutout Figures of Different Forms and Colours into their Respective Colour (Colour Sorting only)

In this condition of the experiment, every details are same as before except a child is asked to sort into the three bowls, cutout figures on the basis of their *colour only*. The child is asked to disregard the form of the figure. That is to say all red figures of same colour have to be put together. A red triangle and a red square are put together. A red triangle should not be put along with a green triangle. Again, as before the errors are recorded. The typical error in this task is confusion arising in discriminating the colours.

D) Sorting the Plastic Cutout Figures of Different Forms and Colours into their Respective Form and Colour

In this condition the child is asked to sort the 90 plastic figure taking into consideration both the form and colour. For example, a red square should not be put along with green square. All red square go in one group, and green square in another group. The typical errors in this condition would be confusion with regard to both colour and form. Both these types of errors are recorded and the percentage is calculated. A percent error is a measure of the percentage of the total number of figures sorted by a child within the prescribed time limit.

E) Identifying the Forms by Touch Without the Aid of Visual Cue (haptic)

The haptic condition of perceptual discrimination, requires the child to identify the form of the figure by tactual experience only. Visual cues are totally removed. On the top of the rectangular box the three figures are displayed in a row. The white cutout figures are used for this purpose. The experimenter asked the child to put its right (preferred) hand into the *semicircular slit* at the end nearest to the child (nearest end of the box is always kept such that it had *semicircular slit* (see photograph). The farthest end of the rectangular box having a rectangular slit was kept always towards the experimenter. When the child's hand is inside the box the experimenter picks up a plastic cutout figure at random and gently places it on the palm of the child, which is inserted into the rectangular box. The child is requested to run the figures on the plastic cutout figure and then say whether it is same as any one of the figures on the top of the box. For example, if a square figure is handed into the child, the child after tactually experiencing it, will have to decide the exact form. It decides it is a square then it answer by pointing out to the square kept on the top of the rectangular box. The child can point out using the left hand, when the right hand is engaged. *No time limit is prescribed.* Once again the experimenter records the errors. It is an error if a child points out to a triangle on the top of the rectangular box, while it is the square which is in its hand.

The child of course can never see what is in its hand. Again the score was converted into percentage.

Prolonged Deprivation Scale (PDS)

The modified version of the PDS was administered by the experimenter through a personal visit and observation of the homes of children included in this sample. For this purpose, the experimental made a visit to every home of the children by previous arrangement. Approximately 4 to 5 homes were visited in a day. By interviewing and physical observation, each item of the scale was assigned a value as per procedure described earlier. A total score on the entire scale was determined. Based on the distribution of the total score a *median cut* was used to select two groups of children representing two levels of deprivation. It may be recalled that on the PDS, greater the score, greater is the degree of deprivation. Therefore scores above the median represent higher level of deprivation than below the median. Children belonging to these two levels were identified.

According to the plan of the experimental study there are 4 independent variables namely age A_1, A_2 and A_3, sex, B_1 and B_2, quality of environment in the school (C_1, C_2 and C_3) and the level of deprivation D_1 and D_2. The dependent measure is the percent error on each of the five experimental conditions of perceptual discrimination tasks considered separately. In addition to the qualitative analysis of data an attempt was made to check the agreement between the results of PDS and the determination of the quality of environment of school by PES. Graphs and bar diagrams are presented to highlight important differences between the independent variables in this study.

The next chapter the results of the analysis are systematically presented for interpretation.

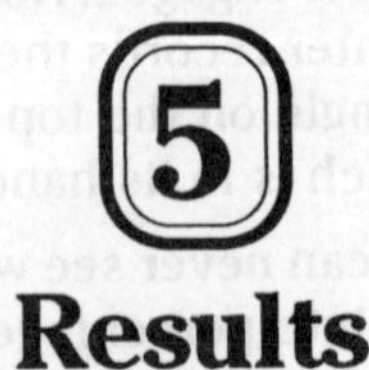

Results

The results of the application of the methodology described in the previous chapter will set out systematically in the following pages. Relevant observations on the results will be also recorded after appropriate presentation of table of results.

Determination of the Quality of Environment in Pre-Schools

The quality of environment is one of the major variables in our study. In order to quantitatively asses the quality of environment as it existed in a school, a special scale was developed. It was called preschool evaluation scale. This was applied to the 26 schools in Tirupati and surrounding areas.

Table 5.1 shows the distribution of PES scores. This distribution had a mean 10.46 and S.D of 5.5. It is observable that nearly 50% of the schools clustered between scores 10 and 14, on the PES.

Table 5.1 : Distribution of PES Scores

PES Score	*f*
5 – 9	8
10 – 14	10
15 – 19	6
20 – 24	0
25 – 29	2

* Mean = 10.46 SD = 5.5

Using the operational definition of the level of quality of environment three levels were setup namely, C_1, C_2 and C_3 and the corresponding schools fitting into the definition were identified. Table 5.2 displays the relevant particulars.

Table 5.2 : Distribution of Schools Across the Three Levels of Quality of School Environmnt in the Sample Selected

School/Subjects		*Quality of School Environment (C)*			*Total*
		C_1	C_2	C_3	
No. of Schools in Tirupati Town		2	16	8	26
No. of Schools Selected		1	8	4	13
Subjects	Boys	6	48	24	78
	Girls	6	48	24	78

Out of 26 schools 16 belonged to C_2 type and half of it to the C_3 type. It may be seen that half the number of schools at each level were selected for the purpose of the study. From each of the school equal number of boys and girls were selected.

Table 5.3 gives a breakdown of the scores on PES, area wise. It may be recalled that the PES scores has hour areas physical setting, staff, equipment and programmes. The total scores in PES has systematically reduced from C_1 to C_3 levels. It is noticeable that the schools differ between themselves widely on area A, C & D. The data ensures that we have here a set of schools whose quality of environment is quite different ranging from poor to good.

Table 5.3 : PES Mean Scores for Different Components Across the Three Levels of Quality of School Environment

Quality of school en-vironment	*N*	*PES Components*				*Total*
		A	*B*	*C*	*D*	
C_1	2	10.50	3.00	6.00	8.00	27.50
C_2	16	5.37	2.06	1.75	4.50	13.81
C_3	8	2.13	2.13	0.25	3.00	7.50

Determination of the Deprivation Levels

In order to setup two levels of deprivation the PDS scale (modified version) was given to 156 children according to the procedure described in the previous chapter. The results of the use of PDS are shown in Table 5.4.

Table 5.4

PDS Score	*f*
240 – 250	6
230 – 240	8
220 – 230	17
210 – 220	3
200 – 210	5
190 – 200	10
180 – 190	12
170 – 180	25
160 – 170	25
150 – 160	18
140 – 150	13
130 – 140	9
120 – 130	5

* Median	= 172.8	Mean	= 175.22
Maximum	= 248	SD	= 25.21
Minimum	= 122		
Range	= 126		

A median cut was used to setup two levels of deprivation. Children getting a score above the medium were designated as D_2 level, and children getting the score below median were designated as D_1. The interpretation of the scores is, higher the score greater the deprivation. Therefore D_2 indicates great level of deprivation relative to D_1. In this study only the total score on PDS was considered for analysis.

It was thought necessary to compile a table showing distribution of subjects in the samples bounded by deprivation levels and quality of environment of the schools. The data in Table 5.5 displays the relevant data.

Table 5.5 : Distribution of Subjects in the Sample Across the Deprivation Levels and Three Levels of Quality of School Environment

Quality of School Environment	D_1	D_2	*Total*
C_1	9	3	12
C_2	60	36	96
C_3	8	40	48
Total	**77**	**79**	**156**

($\chi^2 = 30.54$ df = 2, $P < .01$)

In addition to the above, mean scores on PES and PDS are calculated over the school and subjects (Children) respectively.

Table 5.6 shows the mean values corresponding to the three levels of quality of environment. This was done in order to test the agreement between the two independent measures used to determine the quality of environment. The mean values on both the tools have consistently changed in the expected direction. While the PES scores have decreased from C_1 to C_3. The PDS mean values have increased in full agreement with the interpretation of the scores (Greater the PDS score greater is the deprivation.

Table 5.6 : Mean Scores of PEs and PDS for Different Quality of School Environment

Quality of School Environment	*PES Score*	*PDS Score*
C_1	27.50	156.83
C_2	13.81	167.34
C_3	7.50	211.48

The Results of DAP Test

Intelligence plays an important role in perceptual discrimination. There is a complex relationship among environment, intelligence and perceptual development. In order to examine the role of intelligence, DAP was administered to children in the sample and analysis of raw scores was attempted in relation to age, quality of environment and deprivation levels.

Table 5.7, 5.8 and 5.9 summarise the results. Both in the case of boys and girls raw scores on DAP have systematically increased. There is a significant depression in the scores on DAP as the quality of environment decreased and the deprivation level increased.

Table 5.7 : DAP Raw Scores (SDs in Parantheses) for Boys and Girls of Three Age Groups

Age	*Years*	*N*	*DAP Raw Scores*	
			Boys	*Girls*
A_1	3+	52	3.96 (3.64)	4.35 (3.43)
A_2	4+	52	6.38 (4.29)	8.24 (4.48)
A_3	5+	52	10.35 (6.51)	11.28 (4.52)

Table 5.8 : DAP Raw Scores (Mean's and SDs) for Children in Schools of Three Different Levels of Quality of Environment

Quality of School Environment	*N*	*DAP Raw Scores*
C_1	12	11.17 (4.59)
C_2	96	7.73 (5.61)
C_3	48	6.13 (4.35)

$t\ C_1 \sim C_2 = 2.55$ $p < .05$
$t\ C_1 \sim C_3 = 3.43$ $p < .01$
$t\ C_3 \sim C_2 = 0.56$ NS

Table 5.9 : DAP Raw Scores (Mean's and SDs) for Children in Two PDS Level

PDS Levels	*N*	*DAP Raw Score*		*t*	*p*
		Mean	SD		
D_1	77	8.47	5.44	3.44	<.01
D_2	79	6.51	5.11		

D_1 = Score on PDS < 172.8 (Median)
D_2 = Scores on PDS > 172.8 (Median)

Analysis of Data on Perceptual Discrimination Task

Within the frame work of the objectives and the hypotheses setup for the research study, the most appropriate statistical analysis is the analysis of variance of mean percent scores on the perceptual discrimination tasks. The main sources of variance are Age (A), Sex (B), quality of school environment (C), deprivation level (D) and the experimental condition of the measurement of perceptual discrimination (E). The results of the analysis of variance are summarised in Table 5.10.

Table 5.10 : Summary of Analysis of Variance of Error Scores on Perceptual Discrimination Tasks

Source	*df*	*S.S.*	*M.S.S.*	*F*	*P*
A	2	2530.19	1265.10	36.16	<.01
B	1	0.01	0.01	0	NS
C	2	2615.96	1307.98	37.38	<.01
D	1	682.93	682.93	19.52	<.01
E	4	8440.66	2110.17	60.31	<.01
AB	2	26.65	13.33	0.38	NS
AC	4	725.93	181.48	5.19	<.01
AD	2	400.98	200.49	5.73	<.01
AE	8	898.68	112.34	3.21	<.01
BC	2	49.58	24.79	0.73	NS
BD	1	139.00	139.00	3.97	<.01

(Contd.)

Table 5.10 : (Contd.)

Source	*df*	*S.S.*	*M.S.S.*	*F*	*P*
BE	4	102.71	25.68	0.73	NS
CD	2	687.87	343.94	9.83	<.01
CE	8	888.31	111.04	3.17	<.01
DE	4	398.57	99.64	2.85	<.05
ABC	4	665.21	166.30	4.75	<.01
ABD	2	13.27	6.64	0.19	NS
ACD	4	604.16	151.04	4.32	<.01
ACE	16	4314.56	269.66	7.71	<.01
ABE	8	342.97	42.87	1.23	NS
ADE	8	1272.92	159.12	4.55	<.01
BCD	2	266.58	133.29	0.03	NS
BCE	8	39.79	4.97	0.14	NS
CDE	8	466.23	58.28	1.67	NS
BDE	4	69.16	17.29	0.49	NS
Error	**68**		**34.99**		

Inspecting the table we notice seven out of ten interaction effects have reached the alpha setup (p < .05). Similarly four out of ten third order interactions have turned out to be significant.

It would be a stupendous task to setup table of means for all the significant interactions and therefore it was decided to only setup tables highlighting the Age (A).

Table 5.11, 5.12a, 5.12b, 5.13, 5.14, 5.15 and 5.16 show the means in the interaction cells. For each table the least significant

Table 5.11 : Mean Percent Error on Different Perceptual Tasks against Quality of School Environment

Quality of School Environment		*Perceptual Discrimination Tasks (E)*				
		E_1	E_2	E_3	E_4	E_5
	C_1	2.78	8.71	2.05	1.27	24.97
C	C_2	12.25	26.37	21.32	14.74	58.23
	C_3	8.52	23.08	12.87	5.11	43.67

Least Significant Difference (LSD) = 3.169 (P < .01)

Table 5.12a : Mean Percent Error (Boys) on Five Perceptual Tasks for Two Deprivation Levels

Deprivation Level		Perceptual Discrimination Tasks (E)				
		E_1	E_2	E_3	E_4	E_5
D	D_1	2.35	9.34	3.91	2.33	22.54
	D_2	5.76	7.67	6.72	4.87	23.79

Least Significant Difference (LSD) = 2.788 (P < .05)

Table 5.12b : Mean Percent Error (Girls) on Five Perceptual Tasks for Two Deprivation Levels

Deprivation Level		Perceptual Discrimination Tasks (E)				
		E_1	E_2	E_3	E_4	E_5
D	D_1	2.86	11.54	2.13	1.91	13.79
	D_2	4.79	11.61	9.42	5.69	27.89

Least Significant Difference (LSD) = 2.788 (P < .05)

Table 5.13 : Mean Percent Error on Perceptual Discrimination Tasks in the A B C Interaction Cells

Group			Level of Quality of School Environment (C)		
			C_1	C_2	C_3
A	A_1 B	B_1	6.16	19.38	15.72
		B_2	2.603	19.6	16.625
	A_2 B	B_1	1.819	13.505	12.598
		B_2	10.805	12.756	5.887
	A_3 B	B_1	2.476	6.412	3.325
		B_2	–	6.412	7.585

Least Significant Difference (LSD) = 7.626 (P < .01)

Table 5.14 : Mean Percent Error on Perceptual Discrimination Tasks in the A C D Interaction Cells

Group			Level of Quality of School Environment (C)		
			C_1	C_2	C_3
A	A_1 D	D_1	8.764	13.938	13.150
		D_2	–	25.045	19.199
	A_2 D	D_1	4.390	7.067	5.267
		D_2	8.234	19.194	13.218
	A_3 D	D_1	1.048	7.733	2.476
		D_2	1.428	6.325	6.251

Least Significant Difference (LSD) = 7.626 (P < .01)

Table 5.15 : Mean Percent Error on Perceptual Discrimination Tasks in the A C E Interaction Cells

Group			Perceptual Discrimination Tasks (E)				
			E_1	E_2	E_3	E_4	E_5
A	A_1 C	C_1	4.13	1.61	2.02	0	14.13
		C_2	13.25	18.80	19.61	17.00	31.31
		C_3	9.72	26.17	10.32	6.21	28.45
	A_2 C	C_1	0	8.61	1.05	1.91	20.00
		C_2	5.13	11.35	8.90	4.17	36.11
		C_3	2.79	5.12	7.55	0.88	29.88
	A_3 C	C_1	0	2.36	0	0	3.33
		C_2	0	9.41	3.47	0.95	21.16
		C_3	0.24	4.83	2.55	0.76	18.91

Least Significant Difference (LSD) = 15.495 (P < .01)

Table 5.16 : Mean Percent Error on Perceptual Discrimination Tasks in the A D E Interaction Cells

Group			Perceptual Discrimination Tasks (E) E_1	E_2	E_3	E_4	E_5
A	A_1 D	D_1	7.70	26.62	9.24	2.30	25.84
		D_2	10.39	13.30	15.13	13.17	21.75
	Mean		9.045	19.96	12.19	7.74	23.79
	A_2 D	D_1	–	6.30	2.46	2.89	16.31
		D_2	5.28	10.42	9.20	1.74	41.02
	Mean		2.64	8.36	5.83	2.31	28.67
	A_3 D	D_1	–	5.55	0.44	0.33	12.44
		D_2	0.16	4.88	2.84	0.78	14.68
	Mean		0.8	7.22	1.64	0.56	13.56

Least Significant Difference (LSD) = 10.806 ($P < .01$)

difference at ($P < .01$) is also shown. This value is calculated as procedure described by Ballam (1972).

In all these tables the mean differences are in the expected direction namely lower the quality of environment greater the size of the errors, greater the deprivation, larger is the size of the errors and so on. However the mean percent errors have shown a persistent decrease in the case of C3 level of quality of environment which was rather not expected. This requires explanation.

The data in Table 5.11, 5.12, 5.12a and 5.12b are graphically represented to highlight the major trends. Figures 5.1, 5.2, and 5.3 display the trends in the mean percent of errors in relation to quality of environment and deprivation levels.

In the next chapter the results presented here will be described in relation to earlier studies reviewed and the hypotheses setup for the research study.

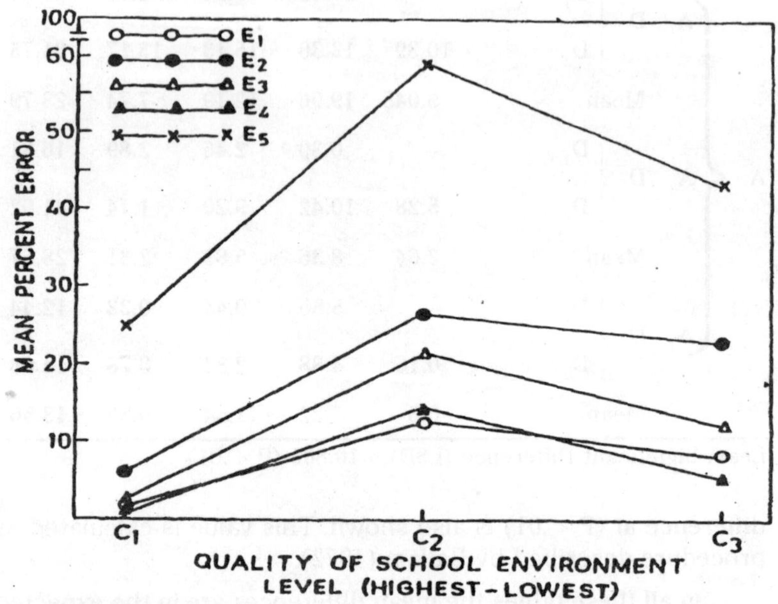

Fig. 5.1 : Mean Percent Error on Different Perceptual Tasks against Quality School Environment

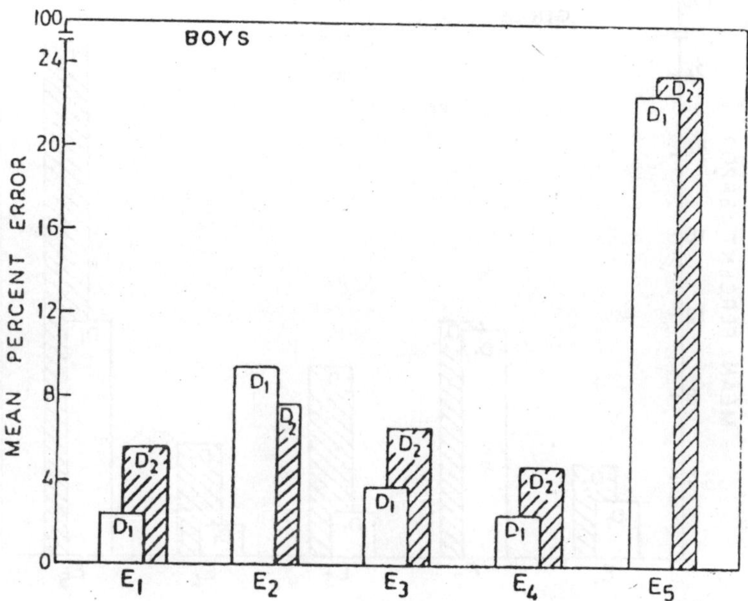

Fig. 5.2 : Bar Diagram of Mean Percent Error (Boys) on Five Perceptual Tasks for Two Deprivation Levels

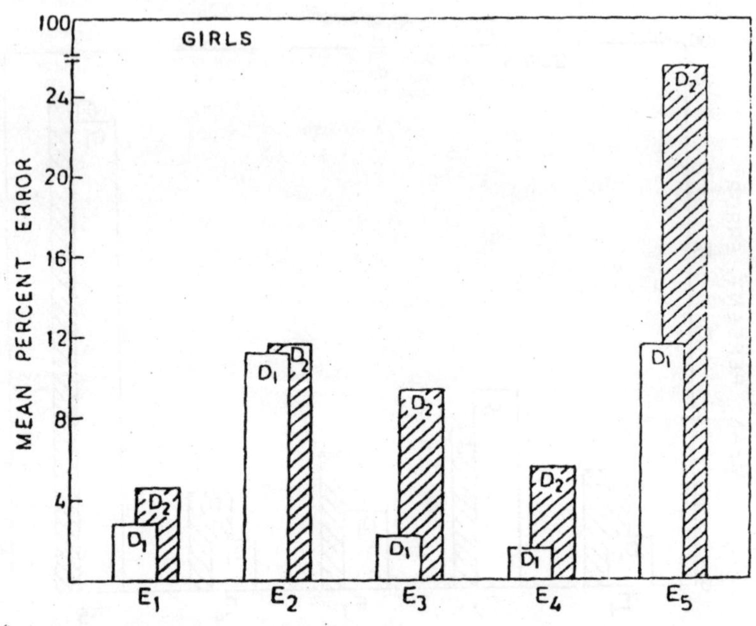

Fig. 5.3 : Bar Diagram of Mean Percent Error (Girls) on Five Perceptual Tasks for Two Deprivation Levels

Discussion and Conclusions

The results of the statistical analysis of data obtained in the present study will be discussed in this chapter. The discussion will focus systematically hypotheses formulated and the existing relevant literature reviewed in an earlier chapter. It is proposed to take up hypothesis by hypothesis indicating at the same time the possible theoretical and practical implications.

The main concern of the present research is to evaluate the effects of age, sex, quality of school environment and deprivation level on perceptual discrimination in children. The justification for such an experimental study and its practical importance have been already spelled out.

Discussion of Results Pertaining to Tools

The question of quantitative measurement of the quality of environment is rather complex and highly involved. There are a number of attempts to develop suitable instruments for this purpose. A major snag is that most of the instruments are not culture fair and requires thorough modification before they are found to be reasonably good. It was discovered that the prolonged deprivation scale developed by Misra and Tripathi (1978) has been developed using modern Psychometric principles of test construction. Hence this was selected as an instrument to assess the degree of deprivation level. Even here the test had to be modified by omitting certain items and restructuring the answer sheet for convenience.

Considering the fact that school itself, has a stable organisational climate the question of representing the quality of such environment on a quantitative scale requires greater attention. With regard to the preschools the investigator could not find any already available scale to measure quality of environment. Hence it was proposed to design a scale including certain logically relevant components which would operationally fit into the quality of environment available to the child. The details are presented in the chapter on methodology and procedure.

The first task in the present study was to examine the results of data on these two tools in order to ensure their effectiveness. One way of doing this is to draw up a distribution of schools across the different levels of quality and check whether such a distribution is meaningful. Another way is to compare the results of evaluation on both these tools to check whether some sort of agreement exists both with regard to the size and the direction of the scores.

Looking into the results presented in table 4, it is seen that out of 26 schools evaluated two (7.71%) schools belong to the category C_1 (first level). Majority of the schools namely 16 (61.6%) belong to category C_2 (second level). Nearly 8 (30.81%) of the schools are below C_2 level and are designated C_3 (third level). It is to be noted that C_1, C_2 and C_3 are in the decreasing order of the quality of environment ($C_1 > C_2 > C_3$). This distribution is as to be expected in terms of their quality of service offered.

The distribution of scores on PES had a mean of 10.46 and an SD of 5.5 which can be regarded as unimodal with a slight skewness. More or less a similar observation can be recorded with to the PDS. The distribution had a mean of value 175.22 SD of 25.21.

The mean total scores on PES are presented in Table 5 for three different levels as well as the mean cell sub-totals for the four major components. The mean scores have systematically decreased from C_1 to C_3 which is as is to be expected. This confirms indirectly that the scale measurement has some internal consistency. (A better index of internal consistency is a split half coefficient which could not applied in the present scale). The more compelling evidence in support of the effectiveness of the tools is from the table of results shown in Tables 5.5 and 5.6. In Table 5.5, the frequency of subjects bounded by two levels of deprivation and three levels of quality environments is displayed. This is a 3 × 2 contingency table in which the cell frequencies have patterned themselves very meaningfully (The size of frequency increasing consistently with the decrease in a quality of environment). A χ^2 test, against the hypotheses of independence between the two will confirm whether there is an any agreement between the two levels or not. The χ^2 value ($\chi^2 = 30.54$, df = 2, $p < .01$) was insignificant and therefore null hypothesis of independence had to be rejected. This establishes the fact that the deprivation measured on PDS has also something in common with the quality of environment of the schools in which the children are found. It may mean that children at higher level of deprivation generally tend to attend poor quality of schools. Alternatively children in poor quality schools, seem to have experienced a greater level of deprivation. At any rate we may safely say that the two instruments have given results which are psychologically meaningful in describing the quality of environment.

The mean scores of both PES and PDS displayed in Table 5.6, lend further confirmation. It can be seen that poorer the quality of environment lower is the PES mean score. The PDS scale scores also have consistency increased with the decrease in quality of environment. Poorer the quality of environment higher is the score on PDS. This is perfectly an agreement with the interpretation of the rationale of PDS scores.

DAP Scores

The DAP raw scores were tabulated age wise in Table 5.7, quality of school environment (QSE) wise in Table 5.8, and deprivation level wise in Table 5.9, in order to examine the trends both in the case of boys and girls. The mean scores have registered an increase which is as is to be expected. The original author of DAP does not provide norms for pre-school years, hence we had to depend on raw scores.

The DAP raw score has systematically decreased from C_1 level of (QSE) quality of school environment to C_3 level. The evidence supports that the intelligence as measured by DAP is influenced by the quality of school environment. The differences between C_1 and C_2 and C_2 and C_3 are significant. This means that children in poorer quality of school environment tend to score low on DAP test. This fact again is not new as Pathak (1966) has herself considered it necessary to provide separate norms according to the levels of environment in which the children are growing up. Earlier study reviewed (Pushpa 1980) has also found similar evidence. Further the DAP scores when compared between the two deprivation level (D_1 & D_2) measured on PDA also confirm a substantially significant effect of deprivation level on the DAP scores. The mean score for D_1 level is 8.47 and for D_2 level 6.5. The difference was found to be significant ($t_{.01} = 3.44$ df = 154, $p < .01$). What is established in the above results is that children tend to scores low on DAP test if the quality of environment is poor and vice versa. Since the rationale of DAP is derived from the general study of perceptual discrimination in children the poor performance of children from poor quality of environment is understandable.

Age, Sex and Perceptual Discrimination

The first hypothesis of the research study states that both form and colour discrimination improves with age. As regards sex a null hypothesis was formulated. The literatures reviewed has pointed out that there are noticeable age trends in perceptual development. However the cyclical shift with regard to form versus colour potency has been recorded. In the data of our study the main effect due to the age was significant ($F = 36.16$; df. (2, 68); $P<.01$). But a number of double and triple interactions were also found to be significant (Table 5.10). The main effect due to sex was not significant. Among the interaction effects the age × quality of environment; age × deprivation level; and age × sex × deprivation level; age × quality of school environment x deprivation level; were significant. Table 5.13, 5.14, 5.15 and 5.16 present the mean percent error on perceptual discrimination task in the respective interaction tables where age and sex are involved.

In Table 5.16 the data is specifically related to age groups and the discrimination tasks employed in the experiment. It is observed that there is a general trend of improvement in perceptual discrimination 3 to 5 years. (The mean percent error has shown a steady decline). Among the perceptual discrimination tasks form discrimination (sorting plastic cutout figures disregarding colour) appears to be the most difficult in all age groups. Similarly sorting under haptic condition is also relatively more difficult.

However the mean percent error has systematically decreased as age increased. The mean score under haptic condition is 23.79 A_1 (3 years); 28.67 A_2 (4 years); 13.56 A_3 (5 years) for children. The difference however is not significant (Table 5.16, LSD = 10.8 P<.01) in the case of A_1 & A_2 levels. The rest of the differences ($A_1 \sim A_3$; $A_2 \sim A_3$) are significant at .05 & .01 level respectively. These age trends are in tune with the earlier reported findings on perceptual development in relation to age, (Gibson and Gibson 1972, Harris, Schallor and Milter 1974, Kagan and Lemkin 1961, Lowee 1973, Clmsted and Sigel 1972).

With regard to sex available the main effect was not significant hence this is not considered fit for a separate discussion. However the interactions between sex and deprivation, sex and quality of school environment were significant and we purpose to discuss relevant aspects at appropriate places. Kagan & Lemkin 1961, Kalyani Devi 1979, and others also have reported similar findings.

The Quality of School Environment and Perceptual Discrimination Task

The quality of school environment was assessed quantitatively using an ordinal measurement scale and three levels were setup. It was also established that there is a significant association between the quality of school environment and the level of deprivation as measured by PDS. It was hypothesized that better the level of quality of environment of school better is the performance on the perceptual discrimination tasks. There is enough evidence in the literature to show that the quality of environment significantly influences perceptual ability of children, (Vermon, 1970, Jenson 1972 and Singh, 1977). By quality of environment, it is referred to the type of material, human, and social components which facilitate a child's growth, by fulfilling the specific needs for growth. Perception and the perceptual ability is product of maturation and environment. There is no escape from accepting the simple fact that poor environment contributes to the poor quality of perception, particularly during growth period. It is on this premise that many researchers have been planned to scientifically understand the impact of environment on perceptual development. The analysis of variance has yielded a significant main effect due to quality of school environment (F= 37.38; df (2, 68) ; p <.01).

However several interactions between levels of quality of environment and age, and QSE × sex × age × deprivation were also significant. Tables 5.11, 5.12, 5.13 and 5.14 present the mean percent errors in relevant interaction tables. Figure 5.1 graphically shows the trends in the mean percent errors on different perceptual task in relation to quality of school environment. It is observable that the mean percent error has systematically increased from C_1 level to C_2 in the case of all the perceptual discrimination tasks. The haptic condition being the poorest (highest mean percent error) relative to other conditions *viz.* C_1 and C_3 levels. All the differences between pairs of mean differences across the levels are significant. There is slight decline in the mean present error from C_2 to C_3 in almost all the perceptual discrimination tasks. This decline is rather striking in the case of haptic condition of perceptual discrimination. We expected a linear monotonic increase in the mean percent error from C_1 to C_3. In view of the present trends in the means which is deviant, it is doubtful whether there is a linear relationship between perceptual discrimination and quality of environment, particularly it being so in the case of haptic discrimination. In a study of malnutrition and intercessory integration Cravioto and others have established a significant impairment in the performance where visual-kinaesthetic integration were involved. Although the exact reason in terms of the central nervous system involvement is not clearly spelled out sufficient evidence is available to warrant a close look into the brain behaviour interactions. The haptic condition involves perceptions of form through kinaesthetic and touch sense. Absence of visual cue retards perceptual efficiency. Since malnutrition itself is a product of poor environment it is reasonable to expect children who have had deprivation and are growing up poor in quality of environment to show poor visual kinaesthetic integration. It is against this background that he hypothesis was formulated concerning quality of environment and perceptual discrimination.

The results of our analysis have shown that in the order of deceasing performance at all the three levels or quality of school environment, E_5 (haptic) ranks first, next comes E_2 (disregarding colour) then E_3 (disregarding form), E_4 (Sorting both colour and Form) and E_1 (Form sorting white only). It is understandable that discrimination of forms based on touch only is rather relatively more difficult when compared to other conditions in which visual cue is available. Delion, Raskin and Grun (1970) have also reported the similar findings.

The next most difficult task is the condition in which the children sorted the plastic cutouts figures disregarding the colour. The difficulty was consistently seen across the three levels of quality of school environment.

With regard to the observation of a slight decline in the mean percent error at C_3 level, two possible explanation may be offered. It may be an artefact arising from an unknown source of error particularly in the case of testing haptic discrimination. Alternatively the scale separation between C_2 and C_3 may not be equal to the scale separation between C_1 and C_2 (interval scale measurement was not employed. This possibility seems to be more reasonable in view of the obtained data. Further to this is the fact that the number of children in C_3 level is roughly half the number in C_2 level. This unequal number might be another contributing factor for the observed trend. Despite these peculiarities there is a strong evidence to suggest that as quality of environment decreases performance on perceptual tasks also shows a corresponding deficiency. This is particularly seen when visual cues are removed as in the case of haptic discrimination. This is further argumented by the fact that perceptual discrimination when the children are asked to disregard colour has suffered most.

Prolonged Deprivation and Perceptual Discrimination Tasks

The term deprivation refers to the condition in which the child is exposed to an environment which does not satisfactorily meet most of the growth needs of a child. Included in this concept are physical, material, human recreational and intellectual needs of the child. The prolonged deprivation developed by Tripathi and Misra and modified by the investigator has 13 areas which are very important to the child. In our study we have set up two levels of deprivation based on the total score on PDS in order to test the effect of such prolonged deprivation on perceptual discrimination tasks.

Table 5.12a and 5.12b and Figures 5.2 and 5.3 depict the data of our analysis. In the Figures 5.2 and 5.3 the bar diagrams are shown for boys and girls separately. Both in the case of boys and girls the mean parents errors have shown a consistent raise from D_1 to D_2 level. The only exception is in the case of boys at E_2 level where the mean parents error for D2 has shown a slight increase. But this difference however is not significant. Deprivation seems to influence perhaps maximally perceptual discrimination under conditions of haptic discrimination. In this process girls seem to be the worst hit.

It is logical to expect poor perceptual discrimination under conditions of deprivation. The available literature points out very vehemently this fact. The results shown in Table 5.14 and 5.16 support this contention that the mean percent error have systematically increased from D_1 to D_2 level at all ages and in all the perceptual discrimination tasks. The increase in several cases is significant at $P < .01$ level. The pronounced effect of deprivation on the performance of girls is some thing not very frequently reported. This is perhaps true as girls have a limited or restricted role opportunities due to socio-cultural factors. It may be that boys some how compensate under condition of deprivation whereas girls fail to compensate and adjustment (see bar diagram of boys and girls E_5 in Fig. 5.2 and 5.3.)

In Table 5.16 children in age group at 3 years, there is a reversal in the trend of the mean percent error under the condition E_5. This is the only exception seen in Table 5.16. However this difference is not significant. It is reasonably established that the deprivation as measured by PDS scale significantly influences the perceptual discrimination among children, thus supporting the hypothesis set up.

The following are some of the salient conclusions drawn within the scope of the objectives and the analysis of data.

1. With the increase in age, performance on perceptual discrimination tasks has improved.
2. There is no significant sex difference.
3. Quality of school environment has significantly affected the performance on perceptual discrimination in children.
4. Deprivation has significantly affected the performance on perceptual discrimination tasks.

Some Comments

A post hoc analysis of methodology, reveals some pertinent observations on methodological inadequacies in the present study. It is though necessary to mention some of them by way of self criticism.

1. The contributing factor of intelligence in the performance on perceptual discrimination task is not effectively controlled. It would have presented a better picture had this been done in addition to mere random selection of children and other controls employed. The DAP test scores was used to analyse the age, quality of school environment and deprivation level effects but not for matching the subjects.
2. Equal and sufficiently large sample of children for different age groups and levels of environment used in this study would have removed certain artefacts observed in the analyse of data.
3. The question of reliability and validity of some of the tools used in this study (PDS & PES) remains open as no special effects were made to establish such properties of the tools. This comment particularly applies to PES.

Suggestions for Further Research

1. Sex differences in perceptual discrimination as a function of deprivation needs to be further explored.
2. Perceptual discrimination in relation to quality of environment in a group of mentally retarded children will have additional information on the nature of child environment interaction.
3. Practical implications of the results of the research may be tested in training teachers of preschool education to plan activities for children in preschools to compensate, for deficiencies, in perceptual discrimination.

7 Summary

Effect of age, sex and environmental deprivaton on perceptual discrimination in preschool children was studied. After reviewing the extant literature reported, the following predictions were made;

1. Both form and colour discrimination improves with age.
2. Boys and girls do not significantly differ between themselves in their perceptual discrimination tasks.
3. Deprivation significantly affects perceptual discrimination in children.
4. Perceptual discrimination based on touch (haptic) is relatively more difficult and is more strongly affected by deprivation.

One hundred and fifty six children belonging to three age groups 3+, 4+ and 5+ years were randomly selected from out of the 26 schools. There were equal number of boys and girls.

The quality of school environment was qualitatively assessed by a specially developed scale. Three levels of quality of environment were set up. The deprivation was measured using a modified version of prolonged deprivation scale developed by Tripathi and Misra (1975). Two levels of deprivation were set up.

Draw - A - person test was administered to examine the influence of age, sex and deprivation on the perceptual ability measured through DAP test. Preliminary tests were made on the tools to examine their effectiveness. Perceptual discrimination task consisted of five different conditions in which the child sorted plastic cutout figures (three forms, circle, square and triangle and four colours; red, green, yellow and white) under different conditions. First task consisted of sorting plastic cutout figures (all white) into their respective forms (E_1). The second task (E_2) consisted of sorting 90 plastic cutout figures (three different forms disregarding the colour. The third task (E_3) consisted of sorting the same number of plastic cutout figures into different colours disregarding their forms. The fourth task (E_4) consisted of sorting again the same number of plastic cutout figure taking both form and colour into consideration. The fifth task E_5 required the child to identify the form when visual cue is totally removed. For this purpose a special box was devised inside which the child tactually experienced the plastic cutout figure by inserting its hand into the box. The experimenter placed the cutout figures in the child's hand requesting to identify its form by pointing out to one of the three forms kept on the top of the box. A time limit was imposed on the tasks (E_1 60s. E_2 300s., E_3 300s., E_4 600s., E_5 no time limit). On each of these five tasks percent error (percentage of errors out the total number sorted within the time limit) was computed. This was the dependent measure. Analysis of variance ($3 \times 2 \times 3 \times 2$) was performed in which age, sex, quality of school environment, deprivation level were treated as independent variable. The mean differences were evaluated by using the multiple comparison test. The results were discussed in relation to the earlier studies on environmental deprivation and perceptual development in children. The following are the some of the conclusions :

1. With the increase in age performance on perceptual discrimination tasks has improved.
2. Quality of school environment has significantly affected the performance on perceptual discrimination in children.
3. Deprivation has significantly affected the performance on perceptual discrimination tasks.s

Bibliography

Ammani Devi. The effect of enriched perceptual experiences through selected books on the performance of pre-school children in simple perceptual tasks. Unpublished M. Phil Thesis, S. V. University, Tirupati, 1984, 40-48.

Aruna, M. and Kalyani Devi, T. Cognitive abilities of preschool children in laboratory and private Nursery schools. Current Research in Family and Community Sciences, 1996, Vol. iv (1), 1-3.

Balaam, L.N. *Fundamentals of Biometry*, George Allen & Unwin ltd., 1972, 173-176.

Belmont, J.M. Relation of age and intelligence to short-term colour memory. *Child Development*, 1972, 43,19-29.

Benerji, and Muralidharan, R. Effect of preschool education on the language and intellectual development. *Journal of Educational Psychology*, 1974, 32, 10-15.

Bernreuter, R.G. Implications of recent studies on intelligence, Trans, New York, Academy, 1953, 15, 301-304.

Bond, E.K. Perception of form by human infant. *Psychological Bulletin*, 1972, 77(4), 225-243.

Brain, C.R. and Goodenough, F.L. The relative potency of colour and form perception at various ages. *Journal of Experimental Psychology*, 1929, 12,197-213.

Brittain, W.L. The effect of background shape on the ability of children to copy geometric forms. *Child Development.* 1976, 47, 1179-1181.

Bruner, J.S. Studies in cognitive growth, New York, John Wiley, 1966.

Butter, E.J. and Jung, B.J. A developmental investigation of the effect of sensory modality on form recognition in children. *Developmental psychology*, 1970, 3, (2), 276.

Casey, M.B. Colour versus form discrimination learning in 1 year old infants. *Journal of developmental psychology*, 1979, 15, 3, 341-343.

Christine, M. and Richard, M.B. Visual dimensional dominance and haptic form recognition. *Bulletin of Psychonomic society*, 1976, Jan, 7,(1), 21-24.

Cook, W.M. Ability of children in colour discrimination. *Child development*, 1931, 2, 303-320.

Corah, N.L. The effects of instruction and performance set on colour form perception in young children. *Journal of genetic psychology*, 1966, 108, 351-355.

Cravioto, J. Delicardo, E.R. Pinero, C and Hindro, M. Mental development and malnutrition neurointegrateive development and intelligence in school children recovered from malnutrition in infancy. Proceedings of the Nutrition society of India, 1971, 10, 191-211.

Crudden, C.H. Form abstraction by children. *Children of Genetic Pscyhology*, 1941, 58, 113-129.

Das, J.P. and Priyani, S. Late effects of malnutrition on cognitive competence. *International Journal of Psychology*, 1978, 13 (4), 295-303.

Davidson, H.P. A study of confusing letters BDP and *Q. Journal of Genetic Psychology*, 1935, 47. 458-468.

Deleon, J.L., Raskin, L.M. and Grun, G.E. Sensory modality effects on shape perception in preschool childen. *Developmental psychology*, 1970, 3,(3), 358-362.

Fantz, R.L. Pattern vision in young infants. Psychological Records, 1958, 43-47.

Fathima, K. and Zaheda, J. A study of concept formation among pre-school children with reference to age, gender and economic status. *Journal of psychological researches*, 1994, Sept. 38(3), 35-41.

Farnham Diggory, S. and Gregg, L.W. Colour form and function as dimensions of natural classifications, Reaction time and response strategies. *Child development*, 1975, 46, 101-114.

Fisher, C.B. Perdinandsen, Bornstein, M.H. The Role of systemetry in infant form discrimination, *Child development*, 1981, 52, 457-462.

Garner, R. Form and function information in young children's concepts familiar objects. *Educational Research Quarterly, Spring*, 1980, 5, (1).

Gellerman, L.W. Form discrimination in chimpanzees and two-year old children. 1 Form (triangularity) Perse. *Journal of Genetic Psychology*, 1973, 42, 3,3-27.

Gibson, E.J., Gibson, J.J., Pick, A.D. and Osser, H. A developmental study of letter like forms. *Journal of comparative and pscyhological psychology*, 1962, 55(6), 897-906.

Graham, F.K., Berman, P.W. and Ernhart, C.B. To study the development in preschool children of the ability to copy forms. *Child development*, 1960,31, 339-359.

Harris, L., Schaller, J.M. and Mitler, M.M. The effects of stimulus type on performance in a colour and form sorting task with preschool, Kindergarten, First grade and third grade children. *Child development*, 1970, 41, 177-191.

Hung, I. Abstraction of form and colour in children as afunction of the stimulus objects. *Journal of genetic Psychology*, 1945, 66, 59-62.

Hurlock, E. B. and Thomson, J.L. Children's drawings; an experimental study of perception. *Child development*, 1934, 5, 127-138.

Hurlock, E. *Child development*. 3rd edition, McGraw Hill Co., Inc. New York, London, 1950, 399.

Indira Malani, Cognitive development in pre-school programme. Report of the 14th Annual conference of Indian Association for preschool education held at Hyderabad, Dec. 1968.

Jensen, A.R. *Educability and group differences.* Methuen & Co. Ltd., 11 New Felter lane london Ec_4, 1973.

Kagan, J. and Lemkin, J. A study on form colour and size in children's conceptual behaviour. *Child development*, 1961, 32, 25-28.

Kagam, J., Klen, R.E. Finely, G.E., Rogoff, B. and Bolan, E. A cross cultural study of cognitive development, Monographs of the society for Research in Child development, 1979, 44, 5, Sl. NO. 180.

Kalyani Devi, T. Colour naming and colour recognition abilities of Preschoolers. Unpublished M.sc. Thesis. Dept. of Home Science, SVU, Tirupati, 1979.

Karuna Kumari, P. Langauge and cognitive abilities of Hindu and Scheduled Tribe children of 3-6 years, Unpublished M.Sc. Thesis, SVU, Tirupati, 1994.

Kimball, M.M. and Dale, P.S. The relationship between colour naming and colour recognition abilities of preschoolers. *Child development*, 1972, 43, 972-980.

Lavanya, Cognitive and Language abilities of pre-school children of Higher and Lower Economic Strata, Unpublished M.Sc. Thesis, SVU, Tirupati, 1994.

Lesser, G.S., Fifer, G. and Clark, D.H. Mental abilities of children from different social class and cultural groups in intelligence and ability, Wiseman (ed) Penguin Books, 1965.

Levensy, D.A. Early malnutrition and behaviour, New York. State *Journal of Medicine*, 1977, 77(3), 350-352.

Ling, B.C. Form discrimination as a learning cue in infants. Comparative psychology monographs, 1941, 36, 36-42.

Logan, M.L. *Teaching the young child.* Methods of precshool and primary education. Houghton Mifflin Co., Boston, 1960, 3-5.

Lowee, R.C. A developmental study of part whole relations in visual perception. *Journal of genetic pscyhology*, 1973, 123, 231-240.

Melkman, R., Koriat. A.and Pardo, K. Preference for colour and form in preschoolers as related to colour and form differentiation. *Child development*, 1976, 47, 1045-1050.

Misra, G. and Tripathi. Manual for prologed deprivation scale (PDS). University of Gorakhpur, Gorakhplur, 1978.

Mussen. *Hand-book of Research methods in Child development.* Published by Anand R. Kundagi for Wiley Eastern Pvt. Otl., Bombay, 1970, 311-373 and 945-1015.

NIPCCD. Pre-school Education in JCDS, An Impact Study, 1984.

Northman, J.E. and Black, K.N. An examination of errors in children visual and haptic-tactual memory for random forms. *Journal of genetic pscyhology*, 1976, 29, 161-165.

Nurjahan, S. Cognitive and Language development of School-going non-school going children of 3-6 years. Unpublished M.Sc. Thesis, SVU, Tirupati, 1994.

Olmsted, P.P. and Siegel I.E. The generality of colour form preference as a function of materials and task requirement among lower class Negro children. *Child development*, 1970, 41 1025-1032.

Patrica, A., Victoria, L. and Stephen. Analogical reasoning in young children, *Journal of Educaitonal Pscyhology*, 79(4), 401-408.

Piaget, J. *The Pscyhology of Intelligence*, London, Routledge, 1950.

Pramila Phatak. Manuel for draw-a-man test for Indian children, Baroda, 1966.

Puspa, M. The impact of social deprivation on cognitive styles of primary school children. Unpublished PH.D. thesis, Osmania University, Hyderabad.

Puspa, M. A study on social deprivation and cognitive development of primary school children. *Social change*, March-June, 1980, 10, 31-35.

Rao, S.N. An experimental investigation of children's concepts of mass, weight and volume. *Indian Journal of Psychology*, 1976, 51(3), 212-220.

Rajyalakshmi Muralidharan. Developmental norms of Indian children 2.5 to 5 years. National Council of Educational Research and Training, 7th Report, 1970.

Reese, H.W. and Lipsitt, L.P. Experimental child pscyhology, Academic press, New York and London, 1970, Chapter-II.

Rice, C. The orientation of plane figures as a factor in their perception by children. *Child development*, 1930, 1,111-143.

Sandeep, P. Class-room interaction and Cognitive Development in Primary school children. Unpublished Ph.D. Thesis, Osmania University, Hyderabad, 1978.

Siegel, A.W. and Vance, B.J. Visual and Haptic dimensional preference. *Developmental Psychology*, 1970. 3(2), 264-266.

Singh, A.K. Social disadvantaged, Intelligence and scholastic achievement. Paper presented at the 14th Annual conference of IAPE, Kharagpur, 1977.

Stein, N.L. and Mandler, J.M. Development of detection and recognition of orientation of geometric and real figures. *Child development*, 1975, 46, 379-388.

Sudha Rani M. The cognitive abilities of pre-school age. Unpublished PH.D. Thesis, SVU, Tirupati, 1987.

Suman, V. and Indira, T. A. comparative study of concept formation of pre-school children from laboratory, government and private nursery schools. *The Asian Journal of Psychology and Education*, 1996, 29 (1-2), 7-20.

Thomson, *Child psychology*, 2nd edition. The Times of India Press, Bombay, 1962, 217-354 and 683-686.

Thripathi, L.B. and Misra, G. Some cognitive process as a functionof prolonged deprivation. *Indian Journal of Psychology*, 1976, 51(2), 129-143.

Usharsree, S. Social disadvantage, Academic adjustment and scholastic achievement. *Social change*, March, June, 1980, 10,23-30.

Vernon, P.E. *Intelligence and cultural environment*, Methuen & Co. Ltd., 11 New Felter Lane, London Ec_4 P4EF2, 1972.

Weinstein, E.A. Matching-form sample by rehesus monkeys and by children. *Journal of comparative psychology*, 1941, 32, 195-213.

Walter, A. and Women. Q. The naming of Primary colours by children. *Child development*, 1972, 42, 1629-1632.

Werner, H. *Comparative psychology of Mental Development*, New York, Follett, 1940.

Winer,B.J. Statistical Principles in Experimental Design, 2nd edition, McGraw Hill Kogakusha, Ltd. Tokyo, London, Mexico, New Delhi, 1971, 775-796.

Wolman, B. International Encyclopedia of Psychiatry and Psychology, psychoanalysis and Neurology, 1977,3, 195-198.

Zigler, E. and Butterfield, E.c. Motivational aspects of changes in IQ test performance of culturally deprived nursery school children, *Child Development*, 1968, 35, 1-15.

List of Abbreviation

A	=	Age
A_1	=	3^+ year Children
A_2	=	4^+ year Children
A_3	=	5^+ year Children
B	=	Sex
B_1	=	Boys
B_2	=	Girls
C	=	Quality of School Environment
C_1	=	First Level School
C_2	=	Second Level School
C_3	=	Third Level School
D	=	Deprivation
D_1	=	Low Deprivation
D_2	=	High Deprivation
DAP	=	Draw – A – Person Test
E	=	Perceptual Discrimination Tasks
E_1	=	Sorting Form only (white)
E_2	=	Sorting Form only (disregarding colour)
E_3	=	Sorting Colour only (disregarding form).
E_4	=	Sorting Form and Colour (both separately)
E_5	=	Haptic
PDS	=	Prolonged Deprivation Scale
PES	=	Pre-school Evaluation Scale
QSE	=	Quality of School Environment

Index